VENEZUELA'S TRAGIC MELTDOWN

HEARING

BEFORE THE

SUBCOMMITTEE ON
THE WESTERN HEMISPHERE

OF THE

COMMITTEE ON FOREIGN AFFAIRS
HOUSE OF REPRESENTATIVES

ONE HUNDRED FIFTEENTH CONGRESS

FIRST SESSION

———

MARCH 28, 2017

———

Serial No. 115–13

———

Printed for the use of the Committee on Foreign Affairs

Available via the World Wide Web: http://www.foreignaffairs.house.gov/ or
http://www.gpo.gov/fdsys/

———

U.S. GOVERNMENT PUBLISHING OFFICE

24–831PDF   WASHINGTON : 2017

COMMITTEE ON FOREIGN AFFAIRS

EDWARD R. ROYCE, California, *Chairman*

CHRISTOPHER H. SMITH, New Jersey
ILEANA ROS-LEHTINEN, Florida
DANA ROHRABACHER, California
STEVE CHABOT, Ohio
JOE WILSON, South Carolina
MICHAEL T. McCAUL, Texas
TED POE, Texas
DARRELL E. ISSA, California
TOM MARINO, Pennsylvania
JEFF DUNCAN, South Carolina
MO BROOKS, Alabama
PAUL COOK, California
SCOTT PERRY, Pennsylvania
RON DeSANTIS, Florida
MARK MEADOWS, North Carolina
TED S. YOHO, Florida
ADAM KINZINGER, Illinois
LEE M. ZELDIN, New York
DANIEL M. DONOVAN, JR., New York
F. JAMES SENSENBRENNER, JR.,
    Wisconsin
ANN WAGNER, Missouri
BRIAN J. MAST, Florida
FRANCIS ROONEY, Florida
BRIAN K. FITZPATRICK, Pennsylvania
THOMAS A. GARRETT, JR., Virginia

ELIOT L. ENGEL, New York
BRAD SHERMAN, California
GREGORY W. MEEKS, New York
ALBIO SIRES, New Jersey
GERALD E. CONNOLLY, Virginia
THEODORE E. DEUTCH, Florida
KAREN BASS, California
WILLIAM R. KEATING, Massachusetts
DAVID N. CICILLINE, Rhode Island
AMI BERA, California
LOIS FRANKEL, Florida
TULSI GABBARD, Hawaii
JOAQUIN CASTRO, Texas
ROBIN L. KELLY, Illinois
BRENDAN F. BOYLE, Pennsylvania
DINA TITUS, Nevada
NORMA J. TORRES, California
BRADLEY SCOTT SCHNEIDER, Illinois
THOMAS R. SUOZZI, New York
ADRIANO ESPAILLAT, New York
TED LIEU, California

AMY PORTER, *Chief of Staff*   THOMAS SHEEHY, *Staff Director*
JASON STEINBAUM, *Democratic Staff Director*

———

SUBCOMMITTEE ON THE WESTERN HEMISPHERE

JEFF DUNCAN, South Carolina, *Chairman*

CHRISTOPHER H. SMITH, New Jersey
ILEANA ROS-LEHTINEN, Florida
MICHAEL T. McCAUL, Texas
MO BROOKS, Alabama
RON DeSANTIS, Florida
TED S. YOHO, Florida
FRANCIS ROONEY, Florida

ALBIO SIRES, New Jersey
JOAQUIN CASTRO, Texas
ROBIN L. KELLY, Illinois
NORMA J. TORRES, California
ADRIANO ESPAILLAT, New York
GREGORY W. MEEKS, New York

CONTENTS

VENEZUELA'S TRAGIC MELTDOWN

TUESDAY, MARCH 28, 2017

House of Representatives,
Subcommittee on the Western Hemisphere,
Committee on Foreign Affairs,
Washington, DC.

The subcommittee met, pursuant to notice, at 2:08 p.m., in room 2172, Rayburn House Office Building, Hon. Jeff Duncan (chairman of the subcommittee) presiding.

Mr. DUNCAN. A quorum being present, the subcommittee will come to order. Before I recognize myself for an opening statement, I would like to show a few clips of the situation in Venezuela. And I think it is going to be on the screen, if you watch.

[Video shown.]

Mr. DUNCAN. I think that is a good preface for the hearing today.

Before I recognize myself for an opening statement, we will welcome to the committee Congresswoman Mia Love from Utah to participate today. Without objection, so ordered.

I now recognize myself for an opening statement.

We are at a critical point in Venezuela's history. Severe widespread shortages in food, electricity, medicine, and the basic goods within what was once the richest country in Latin America have led to starvation, the highest infant mortality rate in the world, and horrific conditions in the hospitals.

Today, Venezuela is on the edge of a complete meltdown. The country has the highest inflation rate in the world, with a falling GDP, its oil company PDVSA, is not generating enough revenue, and the Venezuelan currency is worthless. Gross economic mismanagement, widespread corruption throughout the government, and an erosion of democracy, rule of law, and human rights in the country have led Venezuela to its sad state today. Americans should take note, Venezuela is a case study for the failures of socialism.

This is the third hearing that this subcommittee has held on Venezuela since I became the chairman in January 2015, and we remain deeply concerned for the welfare of the Venezuelan people and potential regional implications from Venezuela's instability.

Venezuela has the largest oil and second-largest gold reserves in the world. But, incredibly, under President Maduro's tenure—and dating back to President Chavez's tenure—the country has become practically a failed state.

Last year, the economy shrank by almost 17 percent. This year, the International Monetary Fund estimates that inflation will increase to over 1,600 percent. The poverty rate is the highest in four decades and the homicide rate is at a 35-year high. Such indicators provide little hope for a recovery absent significant changes in the country's policies.

Those who can afford to leave are fleeing the country in droves. Thousands have gone to Chile, Colombia, and Brazil, seeking food and medicine. And here at home, Venezuelans make up the largest percentage of asylum requests to the United States, with those numbers growing by 150 percent since 2015, according to the United States Department of Homeland Security.

If the crisis in Venezuela continues, we could all have a situation on our hands where we are faced with massive refugee flows and public health threats from rising numbers of malaria and diphtheria cases in Venezuela, and those do not respect borders.

In addition, Venezuela's PDVSA continues to creep along, but corruption and low oil prices have led to slower output. This situation has the potential to greatly impact gas prices here at home, as the United States is the third-largest importer of Venezuelan oil.

The recent news that PDVSA received a $1.5 billion loan in exchange for giving Russia's state-owned oil company Rosneft 49.1 percent of its shares in CITGO is problematic for U.S. interests.

Should Venezuela default on its debt obligation to Rosneft, the Russians would become the second-largest foreign owner of U.S. refining capacity and thereby take control of a critical U.S. energy infrastructure, including three U.S. refineries and a network of pipelines. This is an untenable situation and undermines U.S. energy security interests.

Furthermore, Venezuela's Petrocaribe program no longer provides energy with the same preferential financing terms as it did before. Its beneficiaries in the Caribbean and Central America should continue to seek alternatives for their own energy security, including from the United States' own abundance of oil and natural gas.

Moreover, the political landscape in Venezuela looks bleak as well. While the people turned out in droves last year and spoke loudly at the ballot box in December 2015, giving the opposition a two-thirds supermajority in the legislature, the Maduro government refuses to listen to its citizens. Instead, Maduro has used the Supreme Court and Electoral Commission to nullify all legislative action, and he has thrown over 100 political prisoners in jail.

Maduro refuses to submit to the people's accountability. He has stolen their right of free expression, nullified their vote, and continues trampling on the Constitution and the rule of law.

This month, OAS Secretary General Almagro provided evidence of the further deterioration of the state of affairs in Venezuela and has issued yet another call for the Venezuelan Government to hold free and open general elections.

On March 23, 14 countries in the Americas released a joint declaration supporting Almagro's efforts, calling for Venezuela to hold elections, affirm democratic institutions, and free all political prisoners. The U.S. supported that effort. And while it called for dialogue, it also left open the possibility for further action, including suspension of Venezuela from the OAS if change does not occur.

While I am hopeful that this declaration will result in a change in Maduro's behavior, the past dialogue efforts have all failed to do just that. The OAS member states need to think very carefully about how long to give the Venezuelan Government to comply, as this declaration reminds me of a very similar situation last year in the OAS. It also begs the question for the Trump administration: How is U.S. policy toward Venezuela today any different than it was a year ago?

Last December, MERCOSUR suspended Venezuela for failing to meet membership requirements. It is my view that the OAS should take the same approach if Maduro does not immediately call for elections and change his behavior toward his own citizens.

As an aside, it has come to my attention that the Dominican Republic, El Salvador, and Haiti are not supporting the OAS General Secretary's efforts to promote democracy in Venezuela. If this is the case, I think it would be difficult for the United States Congress to justify continued U.S. financial assistance to these countries, and I respectfully urge them to reconsider and support democracy in Venezuela.

In conclusion, the United States is watching the situation in Venezuela closely. Last year, I, along with Ranking Member Sires and nearly 30 Members of Congress, urged the Obama administration to advocate for the release of Francisco Marquez and Joshua Holt from prison there in Venezuela. Today, Francisco is free, and he is sitting with us today in the audience.

Francisco, I applaud your courage in the face of extreme brutality. Would you stand and be recognized?

[Applause.]

Mr. DUNCAN. He was supposed to be here in the audience. Hopefully, he will make it.

I want to urge President Trump to prioritize the release of Joshua Holt and continue U.S. vigilance in countering the Venezuelan Government's activities in drug trafficking, organized crime, and assistance to Islamist militants. This hearing could not be timelier, in view of today's OAS Permanent Council meeting, and I look forward to what our witnesses will share with us.

With that, I will turn to the ranking member, Albio Sires, for his opening statement.

Mr. SIRES. Thank you, Chairman, for holding this timely hearing, and thank you to our witnesses for being here today.

With every month that passes, we see the situation in Venezuela becoming more and more dire. Reports of families searching dumpsters for food and sick children unable to access lifesaving insulin or chemotherapy are, unfortunately, becoming the norm. Maduro continues to keep political prisoners, like Leopoldo Lopez, under lock and key to send a strong message to those trying to question his actions.

Venezuela, a country with the world's largest known oil reserves, is spiraling into a collapsed state where the people are struggling just to survive. Make no mistake, it is the failed Chavismo policies and the authoritarian actions of Nicolas Maduro that have brought all this pain and suffering upon Venezuela's people. Maduro and his cronies continue to get richer as they traffic money and drugs, while doing nothing to help billions of suffering people.

Instead of focusing on the economy, Maduro is staging mock military exercises and stoking fears by spreading propaganda of a U.S.-led invasion. Press reports show that of the 800,000 businesses that operated under Chavez, nearly 600,000 have shut down.

Maduro's tactics are making it next to impossible to survive. With the recent sanctions of Vice President Tareck El Aissami under the Kingpin Act, it has become clear that Venezuela's Government is acting as a narco-state and facilitating the shipment of narcotics throughout the region.

The truth about Maduro is clear, and the international community is starting to unify against him. The OAS Secretary General Luis Almagro has wisely called for Venezuela's suspension from the OAS unless he frees political prisoners, accepts humanitarian aid, and holds elections without delay.

While a political solution is the only way to provide sustainable change for Venezuela, for the Venezuelan people, the dialogues up until now have done nothing but help provide Maduro a lifeline while his regime is teetering on the edge of collapse. I believe that we need to work together with our allies around the world and continue to insist Maduro abide by the international norms and give the Venezuela people the freedom they deserve.

I am eager to hear how our panelists view the decaying situation in Venezuela and look forward to their recommendations as we continue to grapple with this complex issue.

Thank you.

Mr. DUNCAN. Since this topic is so important to me as chairman, I am going to give the other members a chance for a brief opening statement.

I recognize Mr. DeSantis for a brief statement.

Mr. DESANTIS. Mr. Chairman, thanks for your leadership on this. We have been following now for years the crackdown on political dissent, imprisonment of people like Leopoldo Lopez, but this socialist state just keeps getting worse and worse. They are short on food, in fact, they had the government inspecting the bakeries to make sure that the flour was not being misused, because they wouldn't want someone to make brownies if they are short of bread. They are short on medical supplies. And even in the country that has some of the most proven and largest oil reserves in the world, they are running out of gasoline.

This is an epic failure, and it is really a testament to the failure of socialism, the failure of central planning, and the failure of having a repressive police state.

So, Mr. Chairman, thanks for doing this. We have got to keep on this and do all we can to help the people of Venezuela, because they are suffering at the hands of a really failed system.

Mr. DUNCAN. I am going to come that way in just a second.

Mrs. Love, do you have a statement?

Mrs. LOVE. I do. Thank you so much for allowing me to come and give a statement and ask questions during this hearing.

This is an issue that is personal to me, and I would like to just for the record—I will enter this into the record also—read a letter that we have written to the President of the United States:

I write to direct your attention to the now months-long imprisonment of Mr. Joshua Anthony Holt, a resident of

Riverton, Utah, who has been held without trial in a Venezuelan jail since June 2016, and request that you take action and demand Mr. Holt's immediate release.

Joshua was arrested on fabricated charges of possession of weapons of war on June 30, 2016. He has not been granted a chance to defend himself or to share his story in a court of law, despite being imprisoned for months.

My staff and I have remained in contact with a State Department official since his imprisonment, receiving periodic updates regarding Mr. Holt's condition and treatment while he is imprisoned. We understand that Mr. Holt has lost roughly 50 pounds and has been forced to disrobe in front of guards and deliberately been humiliated. Moreover, he has been denied fair hearing, as his judge has either failed to appear or postponed his hearing dates numerous times.

His treatment, condition, and time imprisoned have taken a significant toll on his family and the community, and I am growing increasingly concerned that Venezuelan officials plan to detain Mr. Holt indefinitely while continuing to deprive him of his due process.

I find it very difficult to believe that a country that has landed a man on the moon, a country that is the leader in this world cannot protect its own citizen from this wrongful imprisonment. And so what I am asking the committee and what I am asking the President is the same question I have had to ask myself: Are we doing for Joshua and other wrongly, innocent imprisoned Americans what we would do or what we would expect our representatives to do for our children?

Thank you.

Mr. DUNCAN. Thank you.

Mr. Espaillat, as much time as you need.

Mr. ESPAILLAT. Thank you, Mr. Chairman, Ranking Member Sires. Thank you for having this timely briefing on Venezuela.

Just as we speak here today, there are ongoing discussions in the Organization of American States regarding the plight of the Venezuelan people and the plight of the nation. I think it is important for us to hear directly from experts on the current political, economic, and humanitarian situation in Venezuela.

Venezuela has been a country that traditionally was known for having access to great revenue and where there was opportunity for an emerging middle class. However, we have seen that the current government has its economic challenges. In fact, according to the International Monetary Fund, the rapidly declining price of oil has hit Venezuela very hard.

Under the Petrocaribe program, 10 members of the Caribbean Community, along with the Dominican Republic, Nicaragua, and El Salvador, had the ability to purchase oil from Venezuela. These challenges for these countries have disappeared. They are now unable to get access in many cases of this cheaper price of oil.

We would like to hear what the status of that program is, and also the challenges of the availability of food and the human rights situation in Venezuela. These are all critical issues that we must address, and I look forward to hearing from the experts.

Mr. DUNCAN. I thank the gentleman.

We are now going to go to our witnesses. And I just want you to notice the lights in front of you. It is a lighting system. You have 5 minutes to testify. It will start turning yellow as it is getting closer in the last minute, and then red. If you see the red, just start to wrap up.

And so we will go ahead and recognize our first witness. The bios and information on the witnesses have been provided to the committee, so I am not going to go into that.

Mr. Hanke, you are recognized for 5 minutes.

STATEMENT OF MR. STEVE HANKE, CO-DIRECTOR, INSTITUTE FOR APPLIED ECONOMICS, GLOBAL HEALTH, AND THE STUDY OF BUSINESS ENTERPRISE, THE JOHNS HOPKINS UNIVERSITY

Mr. HANKE. Thank you, Mr. Chairman.

Mr. DUNCAN. Pull that microphone over. Everything is being recorded, and we want to hear what you have to say.

Mr. HANKE. We are set now.

Thank you for inviting me, both you and your colleagues. I will have six general points that I would like to raise with regard to Venezuela. And before I do that, I might add that I was President Caldera's chief adviser in 1995 and 1996, so I have watched the situation as it has deteriorated and then essentially melted down, as the committee has recognized already.

The first point I would like to raise is that when you think about Venezuela, you have to think former Soviet Union in the late 1980s. You have to put the thing into context.

My second point is, well, what does this actually mean? Some of you have already alluded to this, but the legacy that we face there is one of socialism, incompetence, corruption, massive oil reserves that are poorly exploited, all these things are very common with the former Soviet Union, and the list could go on and on.

The third point I would like to make is that there is one precondition that must be met before all these things can be so-called fixed, because the list of things that are wrong is enormous and the number of reforms that will have to be made will be absolutely huge. And the precondition is that inflation has to be stopped. We recognize this. And I was an adviser to the governments in the Baltics, and also in the Balkans, and also in Latin America. And in all these cases where you have these meltdown situations, you must fix the inflation problem and establish stability before you can do anything. As I like to say, stability might not be everything, but everything is nothing without stability.

So how do you fix the inflation? It is actually quite easy to do. There are two possibilities that are proven to work. The first possibility is to introduce something called a currency board system. I was involved in doing this in Estonia, Lithuania, Bulgaria, and Bosnia, and it stopped the inflation and stabilized things immediately.

A currency board simply allows a country to issue their own currency, but it becomes a clone of the anchor currency. In the case of Venezuela, it would be the U.S. dollar, because it trades at a fixed exchange rate to the dollar. Under a currency board system, it is fully convertible and it is backed with 100 percent U.S. dollar reserves. So in that case the bolivar would be equal to the dollar. If you didn't like the bolivar, you would just exchange it for greenbacks and 100 percent reserves would cover that and you would be fixed.

The next point, the fifth point, is the second option, and that is to dollarize the country and just get rid of the local currency and adopt the U.S. dollar. I was involved in Ecuador when Ecuador did this in 2001, and, of course, it stabilized the situation in Ecuador immediately. And in Ecuador, even though the ideological frame is the same as the one in Venezuela, the performance in Ecuador is pretty good, actually. I have got data in my testimony before you. You can look at and review that.

Now, the bottom line is, well, what should the U.S. actually do in terms of policy? And the first thing is that I would strongly ad-vise no meddling, no direct meddling, forget the regime change kind of rhetoric that is so common in certain circles in Washington.

So the question is, well, do we have any policy? Should we have a do-nothing policy? And the answer is no. There are many things that we can do. We have obligations with the OAS, with the U.N. We have already mentioned the OAS. Things are going on today. And the U.S. can take and use those vehicles to make their points.

The second thing is something more direct that, in fact, hits in-flation. And that is one thing that could be done is what Senator Dole did with Senator Steve Symms and Senator Phil Gramm, where they put an amendment in the foreign ops bill in 1992 that allows U.S. quota contributions to the IMF to be used to help es-tablish currency boards.

As far as dollarization goes, I would just remind you that Sen-ator Connie Mack, when he was chairman of the Joint Economic Committee, was tirelessly working on promoting dollarization. And this helped, by the way, in the introduction of the dollar in Ecuador and then a year later in El Salvador.

The last thing—I am running over, but let me just mention the reality of either a currency board system or dollarization. We just did a survey in Venezuela 2 weeks ago to see what public opinion looked like with regard to currency boards or dollarization. Number one, 50 percent of the public is sick and tired of the Central Bank in Venezuela and they don't trust it. And if you look further into the detail of the surveys that were done, the majority of the popu-lation supports dollarization, 62 percent support dollarization and 59 percent support currency boards.

So, with that, thank you for letting me go a minute and 23 sec-onds over my time, Mr. Chairman, but that is it for now. Thank you.

[The prepared statement of Mr. Hanke follows:]

Testimony

U.S. House of Representatives
Committee on Foreign Affairs
Subcommittee on the Western Hemisphere

Venezuela's Tragic Meltdown

28 March 2017

Steve H. Hanke
Professor of Applied Economics
Co-Director of the Johns Hopkins Institute for Applied Economics, Global Health, and the Study of
Business Enterprise
The Johns Hopkins University
Baltimore, Maryland 21218

(410) 516-7183
hanke@jhu.edu
@Steve_Hanke

Mr. Chairman, thank you for this opportunity to express my views on "Venezuela's Tragic Meltdown." A great deal of the commentary on the topic is polemical, and more-or-less political and ideological self-justifications of one sort or another. In consequence, the discourse is often confused and confusing. In an attempt to bring some clarity to the topic, I will focus on the one necessary condition that must be satisfied before the Venezuelan economy can be turned around. Inflation must be stopped before stability can be established. Stability might not be everything, but everything is nothing without stability.

ON THE MELTDOWN

Venezuela's economy, today, resembles that of the former Soviet Union before it collapsed. Venezuela has the largest proven oil reserves in the world, and not surprisingly produces one major product, oil. Oil production is carried out by a state-owned oil company, Petróleos de Venezuela, S.A. (PDVSA). PDVSA is so poorly run and its proven oil reserves are exploited so slowly as to render the value of its reserves worthless (Hanke, 2017). Venezuela's economy is also burdened by socialist-interventionist structure (Hanke and Yin, 2017). In consequence, economic life is heavily politicized and very uncertain.

Venezuela's economy is collapsing. This is the result of years of socialism, incompetence, and corruption, among other things. An important element that mirrors the economy's collapse is Venezuela's currency, the bolivar. It is not trustworthy. Venezuela's exchange rate regime provides no discipline. It only produces instability and poverty. Currently, Venezuela is experiencing one of the highest inflation rates in the world: 150% per year.

I observed much of Venezuela's economic dysfunction first-hand during the 1995-96 period, when I acted as President Rafael Caldera's adviser (Hanke, 2016). For an excellent analysis of the state of economic dysfunction in Venezuela during the pre-Chavez years, there is no better read than Moises Naim's book: *Paper Tigers & Minotaurs: The Politics of Venezuela's Economic Reforms* (Naim, 1993).

9

In 1999, **Hugo Chavez** was installed as president. It was then that the socialist seeds of Venezuela's meltdown started to be planted. As the seeds sprouted, Venezuela began to enter what has become a death spiral. For a most edifying read—one that gives a real feel for the bizarre state of economic affairs in Venezuela—I recommend Raul Gallegos' book: *Crude Nation: How Oil Riches Ruined Venezuela* (Gallegos, 2016).

To put Venezuela on a sound, sustained economic path will require massive economic reforms. Sound economies require sound institutions, even in oil-rich countries (Kaznacheev, 2017). Venezuela, like the former Soviet Union, has none. So, the task ahead will be great. But, as we learned in the communist countries of the former Soviet Union, inflation had to be snuffed out and economic stability established before successful economic reforms could be introduced.

ON VENEZUELA'S SYSTEMIC INFLATION

Venezuela suffered from an unstable currency and elevated inflation rates before the arrival of President Hugo Chavez, but with his ascendancy, fiscal and monetary discipline further deteriorated and inflation ratcheted up. By the time President Nicolas Maduro arrived in early 2013, inflation was in triple digits and rising.

With the acceleration of inflation, the Banco Central de Venezuela (BCV) became an unreliable source of inflation data. Indeed, from December 2014 until January 2016, the BCV did not report inflation statistics. To remedy this problem, the Johns Hopkins-Cato Institute Troubled Currencies Project, which I direct, began to measure inflation in 2013.

The most important price in an economy is the exchange rate between the local currency and the world's reserve currency – the U.S. dollar. As long as there is an active black market (read: free market) for currency and the black market data are available, changes in the black market exchange rate can be reliably transformed into accurate estimates of countrywide inflation rates. The economic principle of Purchasing Power Parity (PPP) allows for this transformation and the accurate estimates of countrywide inflation rates (Hanke and Bushnell, 2016).

Venezuela employs a multiple exchange-rate regime, coupled with exchange controls. In consequence, the official exchange rates are not free-market rates. To obtain the free-market exchange rates required for the application of PPP, we use black-market exchange rates. Black-market rates are efficient processors of information when political and economic circumstances make the official exchange rate unreliable or irrelevant. The course of the bolivar-U.S. dollar (VEF/USD) black-market rate is shown in the chart below. The value of the bolivar against the dollar has plunged, and with that, PPP suggests that Venezuela has experienced a dramatic inflation surge. And it has.

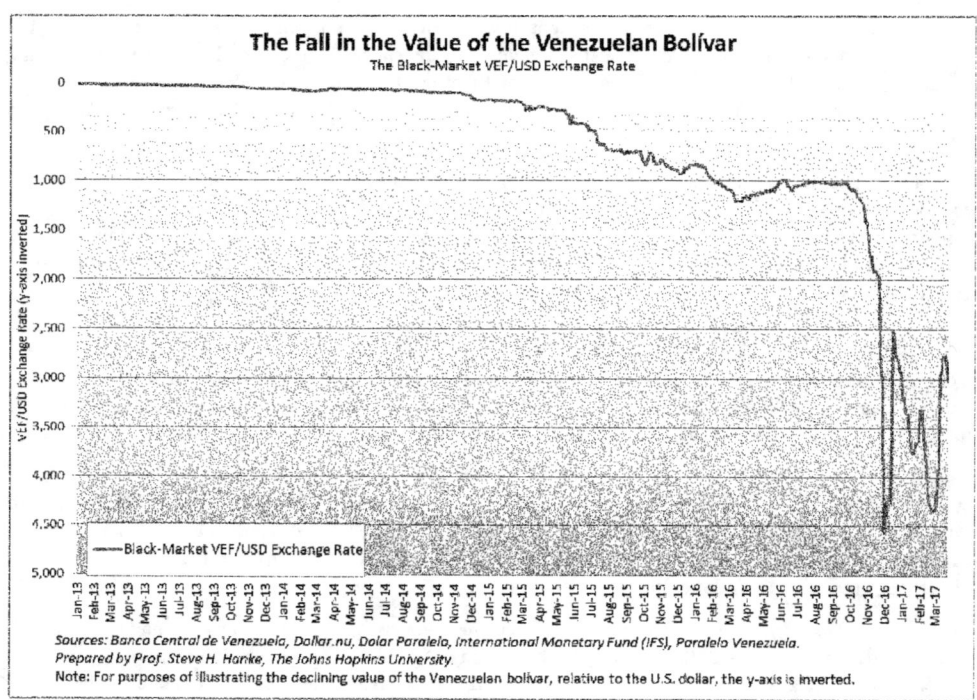

The Fall in the Value of the Venezuelan Bolívar
The Black-Market VEF/USD Exchange Rate

Sources: Banco Central de Venezuela, Dollar.nu, Dolar Paralelo, International Monetary Fund (IFS), Paralelo Venezuela.
Prepared by Prof. Steve H. Hanke, The Johns Hopkins University.
Note: For purposes of illustrating the declining value of the Venezuelan bolívar, relative to the U.S. dollar, the y-axis is inverted.

We compute the implied annual inflation rate on a daily basis by using PPP to translate changes in the VEF/USD exchange rate into an annual inflation rate (Hanke and Bushnell, 2016). The chart below shows the course of that annual rate, which peaked at 800% (yr/yr) in the summer of 2015.

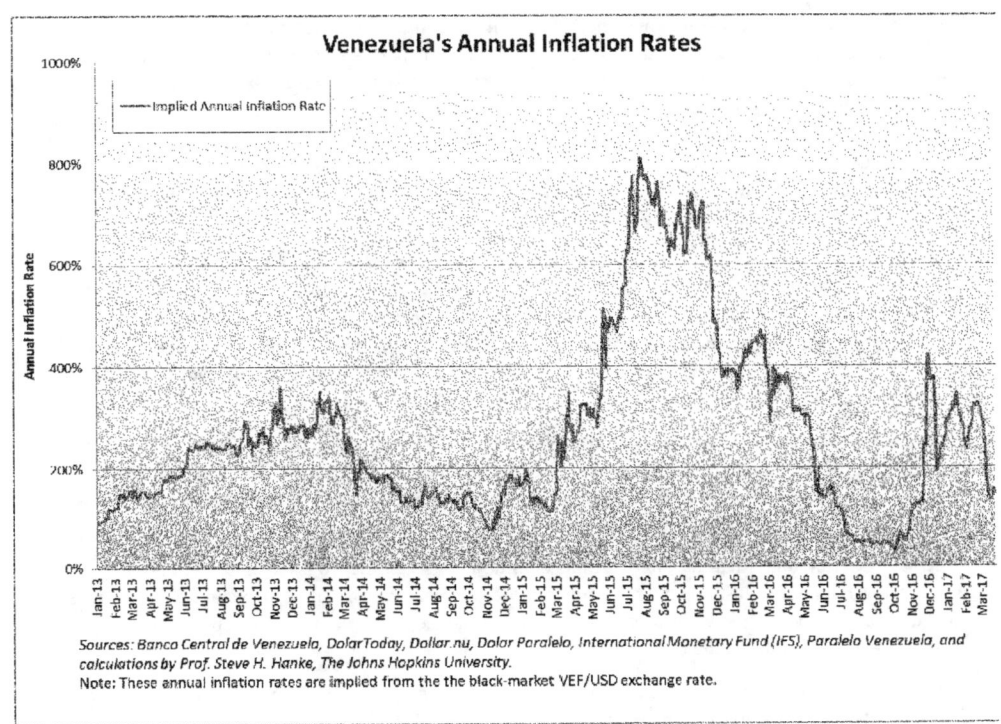

Venezuela's Annual Inflation Rates

Sources: *Banco Central de Venezuela, DolarToday, Dollar.nu, Dolar Paralelo, International Monetary Fund (IFS), Paralelo Venezuela, and calculations by Prof. Steve H. Hanke, The Johns Hopkins University.*
Note: These annual inflation rates are implied from the the black-market VEF/USD exchange rate.

It is worth mentioning that a bit later, in December 2016, Venezuela's inflation became the 57th official, verified episode of hyperinflation and was added to the Hanke-Krus *World Hyperinflation Table*, which is contained in the authoritative *Routledge Handbook of Major Events in Economic History* (2013).

An episode of hyperinflation occurs when the monthly inflation rate exceeds 50% for 30 consecutive days. Venezuela's monthly inflation rate exceeded 50% on November 3, 2016 and remained above 50% until December 14, 2016. The peak monthly inflation rate was 221%, which is relatively low in the context of hyperinflations (Hanke and Bushnell, 2016). Venezuela's hyperinflation episode is the 8th to occur in Latin America. Previous episodes in this region are: Argentina (1989), Bolivia (1984), Brazil (1989), Chile (1973), Nicaragua (1986), and Peru (1988 and 1990).

ON HOW TO STOP INFLATION AND ESTABLISH STABILITY

There are two proven ways to stop "high" inflations and establish stability. A country can install a currency board system in which its local currency becomes a clone of a reliable anchor currency. Alternatively, a country can abandon its local currency and adopt a reliable foreign currency (read: it can "dollarize"). I designed and implemented both currency board and "dollarized" systems in Latin America, the Baltics, and the Balkans (Hanke, 2016; Santos, 2015). I can attest to the fact that these currency reforms always work to stop inflation in its tracks and establish the stable conditions necessary to carry out economic reforms.

So just what is a currency board? An orthodox currency board issues notes and coins convertible on demand into a foreign anchor currency at a fixed rate of exchange. As reserves, it holds low-risk, interest-bearing bonds denominated in the anchor currency, and typically some gold. The reserve levels (both floors and ceilings) are set by law and are equal to 100%, or slightly more, of its monetary liabilities (notes, coins, and if permitted, deposits). A currency board's convertibility and foreign reserve cover requirements do not extend to deposits at commercial banks or to any other financial assets. A currency board generates profits from the difference between the interest it earns on its reserve assets and the expense of maintaining its liabilities (Hanke and Schuler, 2015).

By design, a currency board has no discretionary monetary powers and cannot engage in the fiduciary issue of money. It has an exchange rate policy (the exchange rate is fixed), but no monetary policy. A currency board's operations are passive and automatic. The sole function of a currency board is to exchange the domestic currency it issues for an anchor currency at a fixed rate. In consequence, the quantity of domestic currency in circulation is determined solely by market forces, namely the demand for domestic currency.

Several features of currency boards merit further elaboration. A currency board's balance sheet only contains foreign assets, which are set at a required level (or a tight range). If domestic assets are on the balance sheet, they are frozen. In consequence, a currency board cannot engage in the sterilization of foreign currency inflows or neutralization of outflows.

A second currency board feature that warrants attention is its inability to issue credit. A currency board cannot act as a lender of last resort or extend credit to the banking system. It also cannot make loans to the fiscal authorities and state-owned enterprises. In consequence, a currency board imposes a hard budget constraint and discipline on the economy.

A currency board requires no preconditions for monetary reform and can be installed rapidly. Government finances, state-owned enterprises, and trade need not be already reformed for a currency board to begin to issue currency.

Countries that have employed currency boards have delivered lower inflation rates, smaller fiscal deficits, lower debt levels relative to GDP, fewer banking crises, and higher real growth rates than comparable countries that have employed central banks.

No modern currency board has failed to maintain convertibility at their fixed exchange rate. Indeed, currency boards have an excellent record of maintaining their promised exchange rates, unlike central banks, and this includes Keynes' Russian currency board in Archangel. The so-called British ruble never deviated from its fixed exchange rate with the British pound. The board continued to redeem rubles for pounds in London until 1920, well after the civil war had concluded (Hanke and Schuler, 1991).

It is important to stress, particularly at these hearings, that the currency board idea became engulfed in controversy, thanks to Argentina. What Argentina termed "Convertibility" was introduced in April 1991 to stop inflation, which it did. The system had certain features of a currency board: a fixed exchange rate, full convertibility, and a minimum reserve cover for the peso of 100% of its anchor currency, the U.S. dollar. However, it had two major features which disqualified it from being an orthodox currency board. It had no ceiling on the amount of foreign assets held at the central bank relative to the central bank's monetary liabilities. So, the central bank could engage in sterilization and neutralization activities, which it did. In addition, it could hold and alter the level of domestic assets on its balance sheet. So, Argentina's monetary authority could engage in discretionary monetary policy, and it did so aggressively.

13

Because of these flaws, I penned an article which appeared in the Wall Street Journal shortly after the introduction of Convertibility. In that article, I concluded that, unless Argentina adopted orthodoxy and amended the Convertibility law, the system would eventually collapse (Hanke, 1991).

Since Argentina's Convertibility System allowed for both monetary and exchange rate policies, it was not a currency board (Hanke, 2008). Most economists fail to recognize this fact. Indeed, a scholarly survey of 100 leading economists who commented on the Convertibility System found that almost 97% incorrectly identified it as a currency board system (Schuler, 2005). In short, those that use the collapse of Argentina's Convertibility System to argue against currency boards are using a bogus argument. Indeed, they literally don't know what they are talking about.

The second proven alternative to stop "high" inflations and establish stability is "dollarization". It occurs when residents of a country use a foreign currency instead of the country's domestic currency. The term "dollarization" is used generically and covers all cases in which a foreign currency is used by local residents. Even though other foreign currencies, such as the euro and Swiss franc, are sometimes used instead of local currencies, it is the U.S. dollar that dominates. Hence, the use of the term "dollarization." At present, 33 countries are dollarized.

Countries that are officially dollarized produce lower, less variable inflation rates and higher, more stable economic growth rates than comparable countries with central banks that issue domestic currencies. Dollarization is, therefore, desirable. The accompanying chart shows the normalized values of real GDP in terms of U.S. dollars between 2001 (index value = 100) and 2016 for nine Latin American countries. Three – Panama, Ecuador, and El Salvador – are officially dollarized, while Peru is semiofficially dollarized. In the three officially dollarized countries, real GDP growth has been more stable and generally superior to growth in the countries that issue their own domestic currencies. While Peru's growth has only been surpassed by Panama's, it is less stable than growth in the three officially dollarized countries. The sharp changes in terms of trade, which were associated with the commodity cycle, affected the volatility of real GDP measured in U.S. dollar terms much more in the countries that issued their own domestic currencies than it did in those that were officially dollarized.

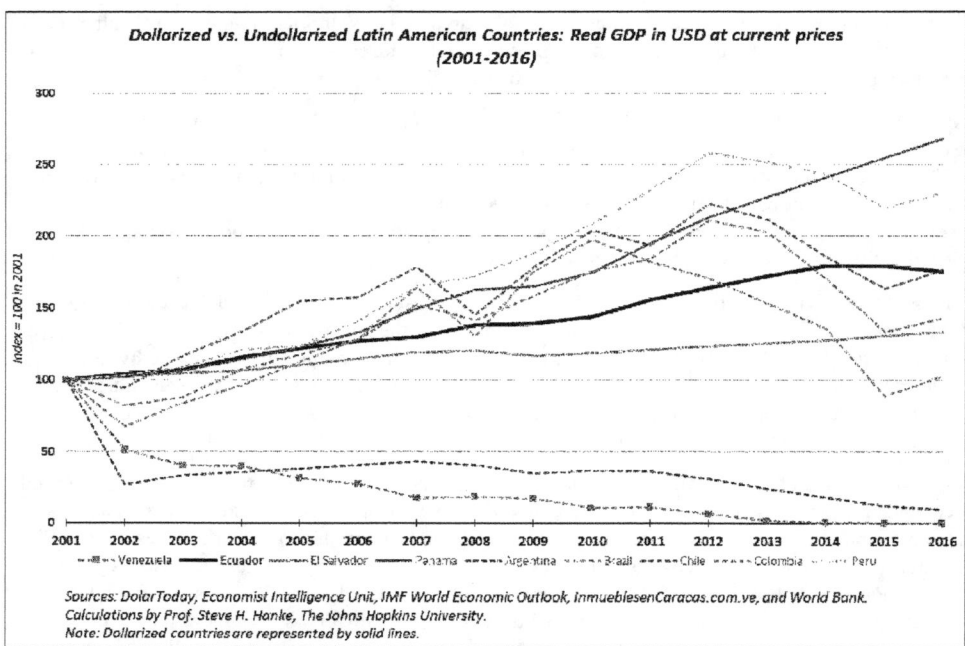

Dollarized vs. Undollarized Latin American Countries: Real GDP in USD at current prices (2001-2016)

Sources: DolarToday, Economist Intelligence Unit, IMF World Economic Outlook, InmueblesenCaracas.com.ve, and World Bank.
Calculations by Prof. Steve H. Hanke, The Johns Hopkins University.
Note: Dollarized countries are represented by solid lines.

A U.S. POLICY RESPONSE TO VENEZUELA'S MELTDOWN?

The meltdown of Venezuela's economy is tragic and of Venezuela's own making. What to do? The U.S. government should avoid meddling directly in Venezuela's affairs. Forget the regime change mantra that has long been popular in certain circles within Washington, D.C. Proactive U.S. regime change policies have a long record of ending badly (Kinzer, 2013; Hanke, 2011; Hanke and Hanke, 2011).

So, should the U.S. adopt a "do nothing" policy towards Venezuela? No. The U.S. has international obligations. For example, the U.S. is a member of the Organisation of American States and the United Nations. These organizations, and others, provide an avenue for the U.S. to be engaged in the Venezuelan meltdown.

In addition, specific actions to address Venezuela's immediate inflation problem can be taken. These actions could encourage either the establishment of a currency board system or the adoption of dollarization. For example, in 1992, I worked with the leader of the U.S. Senate, Bob Dole, and Senators Steve Symms and Phil Gramm to draft U.S. legislation that would allow countries to use part of the U.S.'s quota contribution to the IMF for the establishment of currency boards. This legislation, (HR-5368, Law no. 102-391), was signed into law on October 6, 1992.

As for dollarization, it also has a U.S.-friendly history. For example, Senator Connie Mack worked tirelessly to promote dollarization and sound-money policies when he chaired the Joint Economic Committee of Congress (Schuler, 2000; Schuler and Stein, 2000).

It is gestures such as these that will provide the political opposition the courage to propose the only proven solutions to Venezuela's inflation problem—solutions that would immediately stop Venezuela's meltdown.

In closing, it is encouraging that a recent survey in Venezuela concluded that the public supports both currency boards (59% approve) and dollarization (62% approve). Even a large portion of those who support the current government don't support the central bank (50%) and want change, with 43% favoring a currency board and 31% favoring dollarization (DatinCorp, 2017).

References

DatinCorp. "Venezuela: ¿Bolívar o Dólar?" Estudio de Coyuntura Económica. March 2017.

Gallegos, Raul. *Crude Nation: How Oil Riches ruined Venezuela.* Lincoln, Neb: Potomac Books, 2016.

Hanke, Steve H. "The Americas: Argentina Should Abolish Its Central Bank." Wall Street Journal [New York] 25 Oct. 1991, Eastern ed.: A15. WSJ.com. Wall Street Journal.

Hanke, Steve H. "Why Argentina did not have a currency board." Central Banking Journal, vol. 18, no. 3, 2008, pp. 56-58.

Hanke, Steve H. "On Democracy Versus Liberty." Globe Asia. February 2011.

Hanke, Steve H. "Remembrances of a Currency Reformer: Some Notes and Sketches from the Field" The Johns Hopkins Institute for Applied Economics, Global Health, and the Study of Business Enterprise, *Studies in Applied Economics* working paper no. 55. June 2016.

Hanke, Steve. "Venezuela's PDVSA: the World's Worst Oil Company." Forbes. Mar 6, 2017.

Hanke, Steve H, and Charles Bushnell. "Venezuela Enters the Record Book: The 57th Entry In The Hanke-Krus World Hyperinflation Table." The Johns Hopkins Institute for Applied Economics, Global Health, and the Study of Business Enterprise, *Studies in Applied Economics* working paper no. 69. December 2016.

Hanke, Steve H. and Liliane Hanke. "Démocratie versus liberté Les leçons tirées de la Constitution américaine " (Democracy versus Liberty: Lessons learned from the American Constitution). Commentaire, No. 135, 2011.

Hanke, Steve H., and Nicholas Krus. "World Hyperinflations." Routledge Handbook of Major Events in Economic History, Edited by Robert Whaples and Randall Parker. London, Routledge, 2013.

Hanke, Steve H., and Kurt Schuler. "Keynes's Russian Currency Board." in: Steve H. Hanke and Alan A. Walters, Capital Markets and Development. San Francisco: Institute for Contemporary Studies: 43-58. 1991.

Hanke, Steve H., and Kurt Schuler. *Juntas Monetarias para países en desarrollo: Dinero, inflación y estabilidad económica.* 2nd ed. Caracas: Cedice Libertad, 2015. *The Johns Hopkins Institute for*

Applied Economics, Global Health, and the Study of Business Enterprise. International Center for
Economic Growth, 2015.

Hanke, Steve H, and Jason Yin. "On Venezuela's Supply-Side Potential." The Johns Hopkins Institute for
Applied Economics, Global Health, and the Study of Business Enterprise, *Studies in Supply-Side
Economics* working paper no. 5. March 2017.

Kaznecheev, Peter. Curse or Blessing? How Institutions Determine Success in Resource-Rich Economies.
Policy Analysis no. 808. Washington, D.C.: Cato Institute, 2017.

Kinzer, Stephen. *The Brothers: John Foster Dulles, Allen Dulles, and their Secret World War*. New York:
Times Books Henry Holt and Company, 2013.

Naim, Moises. *Paper Tigers and Minotaurs: the Politics of Venezuela's Economic Reforms*. Washington,
D.C: Carnegie Endowment for International Peace, 1993.

Santos, Tristana. "The Dollarizers." The Johns Hopkins Institute for Applied Economics, Global Health,
and the Study of Business Enterprise, *Studies in Applied Economics* working paper no. 31. April
2015.

Schuler, Kurt. "Ignorance and Influence: U.S. Economists on Argentina's Depression of 1998-2002."
Intellectual Tyranny of the Status Quo vol. 2, no.2, August 2005, Econ Journal Watch pp. 234-
278.

Schuler, Kurt. "Basics of Dollarization." United States. Cong. Joint Economic Committee. 106th Cong.,
2nd sess. Cong. Rept. Washington, D.C.: 349-94. 2000.

Schuler, Kurt and Robert Stein. "The Mack Dollarization Plan: An Analysis." *Dollarization: A Common
Currency for the Americas?* March 6, 2000, Dallas, Federal Reserve Bank of Dallas.

Mr. DUNCAN. I thank the gentleman.

Mr. Dallen, you are recognized.

STATEMENT OF MR. RUSSELL M. DALLEN, JR., PRESIDENT AND EDITOR-IN-CHIEF, LATIN AMERICAN HERALD TRIBUNE

Mr. DALLEN. Thank you, Chairman Duncan, Ranking Member Sires, and my local Florida Congresswoman, Ileana Ros-Lehtinen, for inviting my testimony before you today. It is an honor.

Let me begin on a personal note. I spend my days and nights working with Latin America, by day working on sustainable private sector financing for countries and companies across Latin America at an investment bank, and by night overseeing some of the best reporters and journalists around the hemisphere at a newspaper. Both are based in Caracas, Venezuela.

I began working with Latin America at the United Nations Association of the USA under Assistant Secretary of State Toby Gati and the United Nations Ambassador William vanden Heuvel after special graduate study under National Security Council Adviser Zbigniew Brzezinski and international lawyer Louis Henkin at Columbia University and Sir Ian Brownlie at Oxford, including a stint at the Senate Foreign Relations Committee, where I was a Rosenthal Fellow.

In 2000, I moved to Venezuela to run the Latin American operations of U.S. investment bank Oppenheimer, and 3 years later bought a newspaper company there, The Daily Journal, a newspaper founded in 1945, which also owned other important newspapers in Venezuela, including Diario de Caracas and Tal Cual.

In those roles, I have had the satisfaction of helping to finance development not just in Venezuela, but all across Latin America, as well as overseeing and training a host of some of the region's best journalists. Those positions have also given me a well-placed midfield seat in the battle for Latin America's heart and soul, a conflict, I am sad to report, that the forces of freedom and democracy have been losing badly in Venezuela.

My friends and esteemed colleagues Professor Schamis, Professor Hanke, and Dr. McCarthy will testify to the disastrous results of the Chavez and Maduro administrations on Venezuela. I have been asked by the committee to focus on threats to national security, to the U.S. national security resulting from Venezuela's communist dictatorship, and the country's economic destruction, as well as what the U.S. can and should do to assist.

At the top of that list—it seems to be Russia week or Russia month lately in Washington—in late December, my teams at Caracas Capital and at the Latin American Herald Tribune uncovered that Russia's state-owned oil company Rosneft had secured a lien on 49.1 percent of CITGO in the United States from Venezuela's state-owned oil company Petroleos de Venezuela, PDVSA by its Spanish letters, potentially making the Russian Government-controlled Rosneft the owner of America's sixth-largest refinery and a vast pipeline network.

That reality is made worse by the fact that Rosneft is under OFAC sanctions from the United States, as well as being headed by a longtime Putin deputy, Igor Sechin, who is also a named sanctioned individual.

We made the discovery of Rosneft's UCC lien filing because we were diligently searching for explanations for how PDVSA, which by the end of November was 2 weeks into technical default on some of its $35 billion in bonds, was able to come up with the funds to pay the remaining $440 million of the $4.2 billion in bond payments it owed in October/November and suddenly cause the Central Bank reserves to rise $890 million as well. The threads we pulled uncovered that Russia had loaned the Venezuelans $1.5 billion.

While much of our attention here in the United States has been focused on other issues, Russia's Rosneft has been active in Venezuela as well as all over the world. In the last year, they have acquired Indian assets, Egyptian assets, and this may come as a surprise to Americans who have lost much blood and treasure to liberate that country, but Rosneft is also drilling in Iraq—where, by the way, they are partnered with China. And this year, because of some additional purchases, but mainly because of the sale of Venezuela's 50 percent of the Ruhr Oil Refineries in Germany to Rosneft for $1.6 billion in 2010, Rosneft is now the third-largest refiner in Germany as well.

My father is a career Air Force noncommissioned officer, and he instilled in me a firm belief in the Noah principle; that is, that there are no prizes for predicting rain, there are only prizes for building arks. With that in mind, as I go through each policy I will make recommendations and we can discuss them. Obviously, because of time, we will just stick with the first one, and that is the CFIUS analysis of CITGO.

A preliminary search of the database of the Committee on Foreign Investment in the United States does not show that the purchase of CITGO by Venezuela has ever undergone a CFIUS review. Under the Exon-Florio amendment, if the party has never availed itself of the voluntary CFIUS notification and review process, there are no limitations for the President's authority to investigate a past transaction, especially since the 2007 Foreign Investment and National Security Act includes energy security, obviously something very important to the chairman.

There is more in my written testimony, but because of time I will just conclude that allowing Venezuela to fall further into the hands of drug kingpins with close relationships with Cuba, Iran, Hamas, Hezbollah, Russia, and China, intent on doing us harm, while sitting on top of the world's largest oil reserves must not be an option. Likewise, allowing Venezuela to fall further into anarchy and chaos will only open the door to further death and destruction, heightened regional insecurity, and Latin American instability. If the United States is unable to bring democracy to its own backyard, what chance does it have for bringing it to the rest of the world?

Thank you for your time, efforts, concern, and good offices.

[The prepared statement of Mr. Dallen follows:]

Venezuela's Tragic Meltdown

Testimony

to the

United States House of Representatives

Committee on Foreign Affairs

Subcommittee on the Western Hemisphere

Russ Dallen
Editor-in-Chief
Latin American Herald Tribune

March 28, 2017

Thank you, Chairman Duncan, Ranking Member Sires, and my local Florida Congresswoman Ileana Ros-Lehtinen for inviting my Testimony before you today. It is an honor.

Let me begin on a personal note. I spend my days and nights working with Latin America -- by day working on sustainable private sector financing for countries and companies across Latin America at an investment bank and by night overseeing a staff of some of the best reporters and journalists around the hemisphere at a newspaper. Both are based in Caracas, Venezuela.

I began working with Latin America at the United Nations Association of the U.S.A. under Assistant Secretary of State Toby Gati and United Nations Ambassador William vanden Heuvel after special graduate study under National Security Adviser Zbigniew Brzezinski & international lawyer Louis Henkin at Columbia and Sir Ian Brownlie at Oxford – including a stint working with the Senate Foreign Relations Committee as a Harold W. Rosenthal Fellow -- so it is with great pride that I return to testify before the House Foreign Affairs Committee. (Harold Rosenthal, a senior aide to this Committee's Senator Jacob

Javits, was killed in a PLO attack in 1976, and the Fellowship that continues to this day was created in his memory).

In 2000, I moved to Venezuela to run the Latin American operations of U.S. investment bank Oppenheimer and three years later bought a newspaper company there -- *The Daily Journal*, a newspaper founded in 1945 which also owned other important newspapers in Venezuela including *Diario de Caracas* and *Tal Cual*.

In those two roles, I have had the satisfaction of helping to finance development not just in Venezuela but all across Latin America as well as overseeing the training of a host of the region's best journalists. Those positions have also given me a well-placed mid-field seat in the battle for Latin America's heart and soul -- a conflict I am sad to report that the forces of freedom and democracy have been losing badly in Venezuela.

My friends and esteemed colleagues Professor Hector Schamis, Professor Steve Hanke, and Dr. Michael McCarthy will testify to the disastrous results of the Chavez and Maduro administrations on Venezuela. I have been tasked to focus on threats to U.S. national security resulting from Venezuela's communist dictatorship and the country's economic destruction as well as what the U.S. can and should do to assist.

RUSSIA

In late December, my teams at Caracas Capital and the **Latin American Herald Tribune** uncovered that Russia's state owned oil company Rosneft had secured a lien on 49.9% of CITGO in the United States from Venezuela's state owned oil company Petroleos de Venezuela S.A. (PDVSA), potentially making the Russian government-controlled Rosneft the owner of America's sixth largest refinery and a vast pipeline network. That reality is made worse by the fact that Rosneft is under OFAC sanctions from the U.S. as well as being headed by long-time Putin deputy Igor Sechin, who is also a named sanctioned individual.

We made the discovery of Rosneft's UCC lien filing because we were diligently searching for explanations for how PDVSA – which by the end of November was 2 weeks into technical default on some its $35 billion in bonds – was able to come up with the funds to pay the remaining $440 million of the $4.2 billion in bond payments it owed in October/November <u>and</u> suddenly cause the Central Bank reserves to rise $890 million as well. The threads we pulled uncovered that Russia had loaned the Venezuelans $1.5 billion.

While much of our attention here in the U.S. has been focused on other issues, Russia's Rosneft has been active in Venezuela as well as all over the world.

In the last year, Rosneft has acquired Indian refiner Essar Oil, giving Russia India's second largest refinery, as well as port terminals, power plants and pumps. Rosneft acquired 30% of the Shourouk concession in Egypt and its giant offshore Zohr gas field. Rosneft is even drilling – and this may come as a surprise to many Americans who have given so much blood and treasure to liberate the country – in Iraq (where, by the way, they are also partnered with China).

And this year, because of some additional purchases -- but mainly because of the sale of Venezuela's 50% of the Ruhr Oil Refineries in Germany to Rosneft for $1.6 billion in 2010 – Rosneft is now the third largest refiner in Germany.

(Instead of keeping the money to invest in domestic oil production, paying for the expropriations or buying even food and medicine for his people, Chavez went into debt to buy over $6 billion worth of weapons from Putin, including 92 T-72 tanks, 24 Sukhoi fighter jets, S-300 anti-aircraft missile systems, 15 Mi-35m combat helicopters, 20 Mi-17-1B multipurpose helicopters, 3 Mi-26T transport helicopters, in addition to leftist-guerrilla-favorite Kalishnikov rifles.)

Meanwhile, in Venezuela, Rosneft has partnered in 5 joint oil ventures with PDVSA. Last year it increased its stake in PetroMonagas to 40% after paying Venezuela $500 million to purchase the portion of the venture that had been expropriated from ExxonMobil. ExxonMobil had owned 42% of what was then called Cerro Negro but has since been re-titled in the new name of PetroMonagas to paper over the previous ownership.

My father, a career Air Force non-commissioned officer, instilled in me a firm belief in the Noah Principle – that is "there are no prizes for predicting rain; there are only prizes for building arks." With that in mind, I will try to make policy recommendations as we discuss each problem.

POLICY RECOMMENDATION #1: **CFIUS ANALYSIS OF CITGO**

A preliminary search of the database of the Committee on Foreign Investment in the United States (CFIUS) does not show that the purchase of Citgo by Venezuela has ever undergone a CFIUS review. Under the Exon-Florio Amendment, if a party has never availed itself of the voluntary CFIUS notification and review process, there is no limitations period on the President's authority to investigate a past transaction, which since the 2007 Foreign Investment and National Security Act includes "energy security."

Second, we have gained access to only 2 pages of the Rosneft contract with Venezuela. We do not know what the trigger is for Rosneft to take control of their 49.9% of Citgo or even if that triggering event has already happened. (Our Citgo investigation sparked additional lawsuits from Canadian goldminer Crystallex [which this weekend had its $1.4 billion judgment against Venezuela from the World Bank's International Center for the Settlement of Investment Disputes (ICSID) upheld and registered by the U.S. Federal District Court in Washington, D.C.] and ConocoPhillips against Venezuela, PDVSA, Citgo, and Rosneft under Delaware's Uniform Fraudulent Transfer Act. Those plaintiffs are seeking discovery in an attempt to find out similar information which Venezuela has so far blocked with an appeal to the U.S. Federal Court of Appeals.)

A CFIUS review would be able to access the Venezuela-Russia contract to know if Rosneft is already the owner of Citgo.

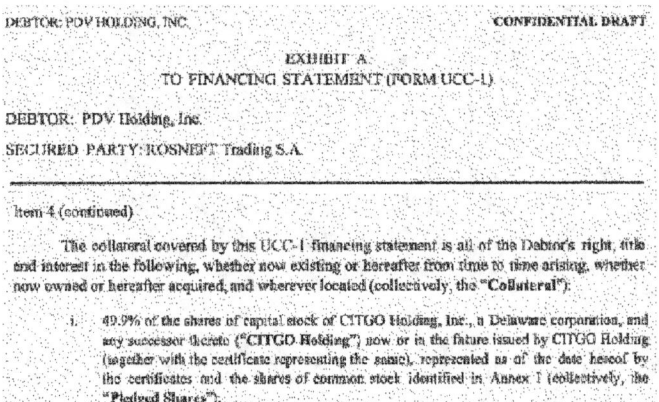

Third, in October 2016, in an attempt to stave off default, PDVSA cajoled holders of $2.8 billion of its $7.2 billion in maturing debt to swap into $3.4 billion of new PDVSA debt collateralized by the other 50.1% of Citgo. It is possible that Rosneft owns a large share of those bonds, with the possibility of giving Russia majority control of Citgo. Again, a CFIUS committee would be able to get access to those details to be able to determine the potential owners of that other half of Citgo.

POLICY RECOMMENDATION #2: REASSESS OUR OIL RELATIONSHIP

Venezuela is the third largest foreign supplier of oil to the U.S. and we are Venezuela's biggest customer. In basic terms, the U.S. has been financing Venezuela's "revolution."

A brief look at the numbers will help clarify the situation.

OPEC crude oil production

According to secondary sources, OPEC crude oil production in February decreased by 0.14 mb/d from the previous month to average 31.96 mb/d. Crude oil output increased the most in Nigeria, while production in Saudi Arabia, Iraq, UAE and Angola showed the largest declines.

Table 5 - 7: OPEC crude oil production based on secondary sources, tb/d

	2015	2016	2Q16	3Q16	4Q16	Dec 16	Jan 17	Feb 17	Feb/Jan
Algeria	1,106	1,088	1,084	1,090	1,089	1,087	1,053	1,053	-0.2
Angola	1,753	1,730	1,772	1,761	1,623	1,674	1,659	1,641	-18.2
Ecuador	544	546	550	547	543	544	531	526	-4.4
Gabon	220	217	219	219	209	209	201	194	-6.9
Iran, I.R.	2,838	3,502	3,539	3,648	3,725	3,725	3,778	3,814	36.1
Iraq	3,935	4,382	4,290	4,396	4,601	4,642	4,476	4,414	-62.0
Kuwait	2,771	2,849	2,799	2,879	2,876	2,859	2,718	2,709	-9.3
Libya	405	391	312	311	571	610	680	669	-11.1
Nigeria	1,861	1,577	1,841	1,417	1,570	1,474	1,550	1,608	58.0
Qatar	666	656	662	652	645	641	623	622	-0.5
Saudi Arabia	10,142	10,406	10,299	10,596	10,544	10,443	9,865	9,797	-68.1
UAE	2,898	2,967	2,921	3,004	3,062	3,090	2,962	2,925	-36.9
Venezuela	2,387	2,169	2,182	2,112	2,056	2,034	2,033	1,987	-16.0
Total OPEC	31,506	32,470	32,168	32,629	33,135	33,029	32,097	31,958	-139.5

Note: Totals may not add up due to independent rounding.
Source: OPEC Secretariat

Despite sitting on the world's largest oil reserves, Venezuela's oil production has fallen below 2 million barrels per day. That is down from 3.5 million bpd when Chavez took over the country.

According to PDVSA's 2015 audited financials, the country uses 580,000 bpd domestically for fuel and power plants. Most of that is sold at less than a penny a gallon -- so at a total loss – leaving just 1.4 million bpd for export.

Costos y Gastos no Recuperados por Venta de Productos en Venezuela

El estado consolidado de resultados integrales del año terminado el 31 de diciembre de 2015, incluye costos y gastos netos no recuperados por $7.680 millones (Bs.528.077 millones) [$16.068 millones (Bs.334.536 millones) en 2014 y $15.193 millones (Bs.92.325 millones) en 2013], originados principalmente por:

- La venta de los combustibles destinados al mercado nacional se realiza a precios regulados establecidos por el gobierno nacional, los cuales son significativamente menores a los costos de producción y venta. Durante 2015, PDVSA destinó al mercado interno 588 miles de barriles por día (MBD) [647 MBD 2014 y 686 MBD en 2013] de combustibles, incurriendo en costos netos de producción y ventas no recuperados para ese mismo año por $7.494 millones (Bs.515.287 millones) [$9.960 millones (Bs.207.367 millones) en 2014 y $14.958 millones (Bs.91.094 millones) en 2013]. Las ventas y los costos de producción y venta de combustibles al mercado nacional, se incluyen en sus correspondientes rubros en el estado consolidado de resultados integrales, de cada año presentado.

Of that remaining exportable 1.4 million bpd, 579,000 bpd go to China. The problem being that **Venezuela receives no cash for those exports**. China has loaned Venezuela over $60 billion dollars (65% of all its investment in Latin America) and Venezuela has already spent all that money and repays that loan by sending crude to Beijing.

Durante el año terminado el 31 de diciembre de 2015, PDVSA despachó petróleo crudo y productos por 579 MBD con un valor de $8.371 millones (Bs.575.589 millones) [472 MBD con un valor de $14.371 millones (Bs.299.204 millones) en 2014 y 485 MBD con un valor de $16.559 millones (Bs.104.322 millones) en 2013], en el marco del Acuerdo de Suministro con la República Popular China (véase la nota 7-b). Los cobros correspondientes a los volúmenes entregados por PDVSA son recibidos por el BANDES, para garantizar el

With 580,000 bpd being burned domestically at a loss and 579,000 bpd going to China for free to repay loans, Venezuela is left with just 800,000 bpd to export for hard cash.

The bulk of that goes to the USA, where according to the Energy Information Agency, Venezuela shipped 719,000 bpd to the U.S. in December, making us their largest customer – and the largest consistently paying customer.

To keep it simple, rounding up to 1 million bpd for cash sale at Venezuela's average price so far in 2017 of $45 a barrel (Venezuela's mix of heavy oil trades at $10 below Brent and WTI), Venezuela is realizing just $45 million per day. $45 million per day in a country of 31 million is less than $1.50 per person. (And I should point out that is before the actual costs of producing the 2 million bpd which is conservatively $10 a barrel).

In short, the United States is keeping the lights on in Venezuela.

At the same time, because of the obvious shortage of cash, Venezuela is extremely dependent on the U.S. and Citgo (which is one of the few companies in the world willing to extend Venezuela credit today) for shipments of refined oil products such as naphtha, MTBE, diesel and fuel oil. In a country where drivers are now lining up in hours long waits for fuel as shortages of gas run rampant, blocking the flow of those fuel exports to Venezuela – which are also used to fuel the army's tanks, jets, armored vehicles and military machine being used against their own people – could be an effective way to send a message.

But if the Venezuelan regime continues to deny its people food and medicine as well as basic human and democratic rights, we should also consider pulling the plug on that flow of money, by either putting a tax on oil imports from Venezuela or even halting them altogether. Those who trample on the free world's most basic norms should not be allowed to profit from access to the free world's greatest market.

POLICY RECOMMENDATION #3: **INCREASE THE BLACKLISTS**

Thanks to the efforts of Congresswoman Ros-Lehtinen and the members of this committee, the House and Senate passed – and President Obama signed -- the Venezuela Defense of Human Rights and Civil Society Act of 2014. With the addition of Venezuela Vice President Tareck El Aissami, who was named a "drug kingpin" (along with his "testaferro" Samark Lopez Bello) last month, the U.S. Treasury's Office of Foreign Assets Control (OFAC) blacklist now contains 12 high-ranking Venezuelan officials, including former Ministers of Justice and the Interior (in charge of all the courts and police and investigative forces in the country), former Ministers of Defense, and even current state governors (who would have been replaced in gubernatorial elections last year but which the regime has blocked from taking place).

An indictment for drug trafficking against the current Minister of Justice and Interior, Major General Nestor Reverol, was unsealed in New York in August. He has not yet graduated to the OFAC list.

A former minister of Justice and the Interior, Ramon Rodriguez Chacin, was put on the OFAC list for material assistance to the FARC. Emails from Rodriguez

Chacin, indicating the degree of cooperation between the Venezuelan government and the FARC, were found on the laptop of FARC leader Raul Reyes, including documentation of $250 million worth of weapons for the FARC. Rodriguez Chacin was replaced by El Aissami, who has now also graduated to the OFAC list, and as the current Vice President, is the second most powerful man in Venezuela.

In addition, because of the efforts of those here in Congress, over 140 mainly, extremely wealthy Venezuelans who have collaborated with, participated in and profited from corruption in the Venezuelan government have now had their visas pulled. Although this list remains unpublished because of privacy concerns, publicizing the banned names is also something that should be discussed, but regardless, that list should also continue to be expanded.

We are all proud of your efforts here in Congress to push the Obama Administration to sanction Venezuelans guilty of human rights abuse and corruption using the Venezuela Defense of Human Rights Act. More names of the corrupt should be added.

Since the Venezuelan institutions and their checks and balances have been hijacked and corrupted, it is up to us to stand for their beleaguered people.

Because of the neutering of the domestic press, it is the foreign press and the foreign press reporters in Venezuela that are left to do much of the work of getting the word out, which they do at great risk.

Congress, the Administration, Prosecutors and the Courts here must continue to do the heavy-lifting of fighting and prosecuting the corruption and continue to provide evidence of the corruption, so that Venezuelans can see the evidence of the betrayal, deceit and criminality of their leaders with their own eyes.

Those who trample the most basic tenets of the West's rule of law – from the universal rights of man and human rights to those against bribery, corruption, drug trafficking, theft, money laundering, and murder -- must not be allowed to enjoy the economic and political benefits that flow from our society's diligence in upholding that moral core curriculum.

CONCLUSION

Allowing Venezuela to fall further into the hands of drug kingpins -- with close relationships with Cuba, Iran, Hamas, Hezbollah, Russia and China -- intent on doing us harm while sitting on top of the world's largest oil reserves must not be an option.

Likewise, allowing Venezuela to fall further into anarchy and chaos will only open the door to further death and destruction, heightening regional insecurity and Latin American instability.

If the United States is unable to bring democracy to its own backyard, what chance does it have for bringing it to the rest of the world?

Thank you for your time, efforts, concern and good offices.

I am happy to elaborate further on any of these strategies and others.

Mr. Duncan. Thank you.
Mr. Schamis.

STATEMENT OF HECTOR SCHAMIS, PH.D., ADJUNCT PROFESSOR, WALSH SCHOOL OF FOREIGN SERVICE, GEORGETOWN UNIVERSITY

Mr. Schamis. Thank you, Mr. Chairman, Ranking Member, and members of the committee. Thank you for this session.

To say that there is a tragic meltdown in Venezuela is perhaps an understatement, and I will try to highlight why the political, social, and economic dimensions and the security for the hemisphere are involved in this tragic meltdown.

The constitutional order has broken down in Venezuela. The National Assembly is in the hands of the opposition after the landslide victory you, Mr. Chairman, highlighted, in December 2015, but ever since, it has lost all capacity to approve the budget, to legislate. It has even lost parliamentary immunity. Just this morning, the Supreme Court has ruled an across-the-board suspension of parliamentary immunity for the members of the National Assembly, how Congress is known in Venezuela.

There are political prisoners with no rights. Torture has been reported. Francisco Marquez is someone we just mentioned. And the number of prisoners is 115 today. All of these while the government was allegedly maintaining a dialogue, discussing the liberation of political prisoners, the release of political prisoners.

The sphere of political rights has shrunk to the point of extinction. The government has suspended elections indefinitely. There are supposed to be this year regional elections. They will not happen. And it has canceled the right of the Venezuelan people to recall its President, the recall referendum. There is no separation of powers nor checks and balances. Venezuela is under a dictatorship. There is a deep economic and social crisis that has been mentioned already. I don't want to go too much into that. The monetary base has expanded to 236 percent. Inflation is the highest in the world. The population is below the poverty line at 82 percent, and 52 percent under extreme poverty.

All of this has entailed a deep humanitarian crisis. The basic basket is worth 15.3 minimum wages, 9.6 million people eat two or less meals a day, and there have been reports of weight loss and protein consumption decline. What we saw before shows people scavenging in garbage cans. There have been reports of children dying by ingesting poison Yuca, the tuber that is poisonous. People in hospitals have to provide their own medicines and everything they need for their treatment because there are no drugs, whether that is painkillers, antibiotics, let alone drugs for cancer treatment. The collapse of the public health system, we have to highlight, has been much worsened by the government's incompetence and its criminal refusal, I want to add, to accept international humanitarian aid. The Maduro government talks about foreign invasion. They reject the foreign invasion of the Red Cross to assist this humanitarian crisis.

There is corruption and crime. As the U.S. Department of State has reported, the Vice President has been named, designated a kingpin narcotics trafficker. The freezing of assets of the Vice

President amounts to $3 billion. This is not the first time this has happened. Previous high officials of the government have also been identified and charged with drug trafficking. And the nephews of the First Lady have been tried and are expecting conviction in New York.

Inevitably, lawlessness from above breeds lawlessness from below. Venezuela experienced 28,000 killings and violent acts throughout the country in 2015. Caracas is the most violent city on Earth, with a murder rate of 120 per 100,000 inhabitants.

In my testimony, in my written testimony, I make a call for action. We are in front of a narco-state that entails risks for the security of the hemisphere, the U.S. and the neighbors. Today, the Colombian Senate discussed this morning the existence of 1 million refugees in Colombia alone. Venezuela is a large country, 30 million people, bordering Brazil, Colombia, Guyana, and with a coast in the Caribbean. Panama has begun to deny visas to Venezuelans. And this humanitarian crisis that you see normally in situations of war is happening in Venezuela as well.

I entirely support the call for the invocation of the Inter-American Democratic Charter. The Senate has passed a resolution, the U.S. Senate has passed a resolution, Resolution 35, making that call as well. You just made that convocation, you convoked to that, and Mr. Duncan as well. And we need to certainly accomplish more cohesion. We need better collective action in the hemisphere. The OAS is the natural place and Secretary Almagro is certainly leading the way with that.

We started last year with Article 20, which calls for an assessment of the Venezuelan situation, but Senator General Almagro has now invoked Article 21, which calls for a suspension of a country which has broken down the constitutional arrangement. We need to put words and actions together. Countries sitting on the fence must come on this side and put enough pressure on the Venezuelan regime to change, to call for elections, to release political prisoners, and to have a timetable for attending to the grave humanitarian crisis that the Venezuelans are suffering.

Thank you very much.

[The prepared statement of Mr. Schamis follows:]

March 28, 2017

Hector E. Schamis

Adjunct Professor, Walsh School of Foreign Service, Georgetown University,
Columnist *El País* (Madrid) and Senior Advisor to Luis Almagro, Secretary General of the
Organization of American States

Testimony for the session "Venezuela's Tragic Meltdown"

Mr. Chairman, Ranking Members, Members of the Committee, thank you for the invitation to testify today. I appreciate your interest in this important subject. All views presented here are solely mine, and do not reflect the views of any of the institutions I am affiliated with.

To say that Venezuela is in a crisis is an understatement; its depth and reach cannot be ignored any longer. This crisis has implications not only for Venezuela and its people but also for the neighboring countries and the security of the hemisphere as a whole. It is a multidimensional disaster: political, economic, humanitarian, and of law and order. It truly is a nightmare at the door, as this session is entitled, a meltdown that begs for action.

The international community must act using its available institutional tools, its diplomatic resources and its normative architecture, as specified by international and human rights law and the regional agreements that bind us. The rights, health, safety and lives of the Venezuelan people merits nothing less. They need help, and we need to have the courage to stand up to this appalling injustice.

The Breakdown of the Constitutional Order

For quite some time, there has been a staunch effort on the part of President Maduro's government to deviate from the constitutional procedures it is required to follow. This practice has reached a critical point today, a peak at which a complete lack of accountability renders the Constitution meaningless.

In December 2015 a midterm election gave the opposition MUD (United Democratic Table) a landslide victory, attaining its own qualified majority in the National Assembly, the Venezuelan unicameral legislative branch. Since then, the government has tried to neutralize the legislature with a sophisticated and never-ending menu of manipulation, including packing the Supreme Court with cronies and using it to rule unconstitutional virtually every piece of legislation.

As a result, a series of anomalous procedures and decisions have become routine. The Venezuelan Congress does not approve the budget nor can it appropriate resources for the Executive branch or government agencies. The government unilaterally makes these decisions via executive decree authority, in turn validated by the Supreme Court.

Congress has been stripped of its responsibility over the contracting of foreign debt, a process that the Executive has undertaken unilaterally and unconstitutionally, including the issuing of swaps, bonds and other strategies of debt restructuring by the state-owned oil company PDVSA.

Because of these anomalies, Congress is unable to oversee the other branches of government, nominate judges, confirm appointments, and supervise mining and oil concessions. Last but not least, a number of members of Congress have been arrested and denied passports to travel, in violation of their civil rights and their parliamentary immunity.

In sum, while the legislative branch remains open, it has been neutered, one may say, by the combined actions of the Executive and Judicial branches through a series of decisions that should be seen as equivalent to a coup d'état.

Individual rights are thus non-existent. The security apparatus detains people at will. The number of political prisoners has increased throughout the last year, reaching 115 today. All this while the government was carrying out a presumed—but obviously insincere—dialogue with the opposition for their release. Students, professors, journalists and political leaders, among them, several of those prisoners have been convicted with false evidence, as was recognized by their own prosecutors. Most remain detained without trial. Those in custody often report being tortured. And prisoners in need of medical care rarely receive it.[1]

The sphere of political rights, that was robust until 2015, has shrunk to the point of extinction. The government has cancelled the right of the Venezuelan people to recall their president—as specified by the Constitution—and has suspended gubernatorial elections indefinitely.

The type and extent of civil and political rights withdrawn amount to a breakdown of constitutional democracy. The absence of separation of powers and the erosion of checks and balances are, in fact, defining characteristic of authoritarianism. Add that the ruling party has been in office for eighteen consecutive years and that indefinite reelection is legal. Plain and simple, Venezuela is under a dictatorship.

Economic and Social Crisis

Venezuela has one of the most abundant geological endowments in the world. The state-owned oil company PDVSA represents over 90% of total exports and 12% of its GDP. During the last decade of very high prices, the country wasted a unique opportunity to increase investment and production. Instead, production steadily declined due to lack of investment, incompetence, and corruption.

Oil production decreased 253 kbpd (thousand barrel per day) or 8% between 2010 and 2015. In particular, production fell 24.3% and 15.8% in the traditional East and West regions (light, medium-grade crude), and only rose 12.0% in the Orinoco Oil Belt (heavy, extra-heavy crude). Production in

---

[1] Foro Penal Venezolano https://foropenal.com

fields solely operated by PDVSA declined 27.5% while fields operated by joint ventures increased 42.3%.[2]

PDVSA's debt service increased almost tenfold to $10.2bn in 2010-2015 while total financial debt rose 75% to roughly $45bn. PDVSA was noted to have an ongoing struggle to raise capital expenditures to halt the decline in production, let alone meet production targets. Its numerous operational challenges should also be considered to explain this decline: input shortages, drilling inefficiencies, inadequacy of gas and energy facilities, insufficient downstream infrastructure (refiners, upgraders, etc), safety, environment and crime related risks, and deficits related to corporate governance and industrial policy.

Having exhausted foreign and domestic debt issuance and choosing to forego international assistance, the government has consistently relied on deficit monetization. Between 2013 and 2015 average deficit monetization sat at 13% of GDP. In 2016 the monetary financing of the deficit was associated to an increase in the monetary base of 236%. It should be noted that the total increase in "direct loans" to PDVSA outlined above was 22% larger than the total increase in the monetary base, which speaks to the reliance on monetary financing.

Debt service appears unsustainable given the lack of access to international finance. Public external debt is at least $130 billion, equivalent to 5.8 years of exports under reasonable assumptions for oil prices in the short term. The Government continues to sustain major regressive implicit subsidies for gasoline, utilities and foreign exchange. Conservative estimates put these subsidies at $14 to $19 billion. Additionally, the combined pressures of recession and inflation are generating a significant collapse in tax revenues.

So far the government managed to stay in good terms with its creditors. It negotiated new conditions on oil payments with China, its largest foreign creditor. It has swapped $3 billion in PDVSA bonds for longer maturities and has raised $1.5 billion from Russia's oil company Rosneft. It has also issued additional $5 billion for undisclosed buyers. Without a dramatic increase in oil price, Venezuela's capacity to service its debt will continue declining. For several financial analysts, default is inevitable.

At the same time, Venezuela's reserves are crashing to a new low below $10.5 billion. The Central Bank reports that they closed 2016 with $7.7 billion in gold reserves, using their pricing methodology of $1,272.42 an ounce. That level is down $2.3 billion from the $10.04 billion in gold reported in Venezuela's 2015 financials, which used a lower gold price of $1,140.43. Venezuela's gold has now fallen to almost half of what it was in just two years, as Venezuela reported that it started 2015 with $14.6 billion in gold.[3]

---

[2] Economic Data from "Weathering Collapse: An Assessment of the Financial and Operational Situation of the Venezuelan Oil Industry," Hernandez, I. & Monaldi, F, Center for International Development at Harvard University, November 2016, http://growthlab.cid.harvard.edu/files/growthlab/files/venezuela_oil_cidwp_327.pdf and "Microeconomic Binding Constraints on Private Investment and Growth in Venezuela," Richard Obuchi, Bárbara Lira and Daniel Raguá, Center for International Development, Harvard University, October 2016, http://growthlab.cid.harvard.edu/files/growthlab/files/microconstraints_venezuela.pdf
[3] Barron's: 2 Experts Question Venezuela's Gold, Cash Stats, http://www.venezuelaopportunityfund.com/tag/russ-dallen/

The country is plagued by the world's highest inflation, an annual 800%. The 100-bolivar note, worth less than 10 cents, was replaced last December. Venezuelans waited in long lines to exchange their soon-to-be-worthless notes, but they went out of circulation before the replacement bills had arrived at banks or ATMs. People were forced to rely on credit cards or bank transfers, out of reach for the very poor, or to try to make purchases with bundles of hard-to-find smaller bills often worth less than a penny each.

Venezuela is thus a nation of broke millionaires, a result of the misguided fiscal and monetary policy of an abusive government. Given these conditions, the country's population is facing a critical situation, bordering a humanitarian crisis that demands urgent response. Recent independent studies put the share of population under the poverty line at 82% and the share of population under extreme poverty at 52%. These are alarming figures that represent historic highs.

These same studies report that existing social programs are poorly targeted. 72% of the population mention that they are not covered by any social program, and out of the 28% that claim they are benefited by a social program only 40% are poor. [4]

The complete collapse of the social safety net is particularly worrisome given the complex fiscal outlook, the absence of timely reforms that could trigger an economic recovery and the decision to prioritize the fulfillment of potentially unsustainable debt service over other policy goals.

A Humanitarian Catastrophe

Access to food and health care has worsened dramatically in Venezuela, a situation that must be deemed alarming if not tragic. Urgent action on the part of the government, international organizations, and relief institutions is needed.

In January 2017, the basic food basket had increased 14% in relation to December 2016, and 481% from a year before. The purchase of the basic basket is worth 15.3 minimum wages. [5]

In addition to high inflation, access to food has been compromised by shortages and undersupply of a long list of staples. From dairy products to beef, from oil to flour, deodorant, soap, tooth paste and many more, present a situation of scarcity. [6]

Venezuelans who reside overseas pack their suitcases with basic need products for their families when they visit. Food security is a luxury that only 6.7% of households enjoy. About 9,6 million people eat two or less meals a day. The nutritional pattern has experienced a dramatic change: garden produce and tubers have displaced foods with higher protein content. This is consistent with

---

[4] ENCOVI 2016: http://www.rectorado.usb.ve/vida/sites/default/files/encovi/2016/UCV-UCAB-USB.%20ENCOVI%202016.%20Pobreza.pdf
[5] Centro de Documentación y Análisis Social de la Federación Venezolana de Maestros, https://www.derechos.org.ve/actualidad/cendas-fvm-el-precio-de-la-canasta-alimentaria-supero-los-seiscientos-mil-bolivares
[6] Ibid.

the report that 73% of the population have experienced weight loss averaging 8.7 kilograms (20 pounds) during the past year.[7]

Faced with a food basket that has become gradually unavailable, Venezuelans in poverty have been substituting products for cheaper ones and the very poorest increasingly looking for food in garbage cans. There has been a number of stories reported by the press about children dying by ingesting cassava without supervision. *Yuca* in Venezuela, the tuber has a sweet but also a bitter, poisonous, variety that can be deadly.[8]

Social media performs many functions in the world: information, entertainment, political debate, and many more. In Venezuela, Twitter, Facebook and other platforms have also become a virtual pharmacy, where people implore for undersupplied drug and others offer to even donate it. Shortages range from expensive drugs for cancer treatment to more routine antibiotics and regular painkillers. Many people have died of an untreated cancer or an unmedicated infection.

According to the medical profession, hospitals and clinics only possess about 3% of the medical supplies needed. Thus, to be treated patients must bring the materials themselves: drugs, gauze, intravenous serum, and the like, in addition to the food for their stay.[9] Others reported that hospitals lack supplies, water, and cleaning materials. They experience power outages and their equipment is damaged, often to a point of no return.[10]

Infant mortality has increased rapidly. According to journalistic reports the rate of infant mortality is 18.6 per one thousand children born alive. That number is above the indicator of 15.4 that UNICEF estimates for Syria, a country vastly damaged by war. In the first five months of 2016, 4,074 babies died before turning one year old, 18.5% more than in the same period for 2015, and 50% higher than the same interval of time in 2012.[11]

Diseases once controlled or eradicated have made an alarming comeback. Experts project for this year about 250 thousand cases of malaria, and between 350 and 500 hundred cases of diphtheria, which had been eradicated in the past. In what amounts to a total collapse of the public health system, the situation has been much worsened by the incompetence of the government and its criminal refusal to accept international humanitarian aid.[12]

---

[7] Encuesta sobre Condiciones de Vida Venezuela 2016 Alimentación. http://observatoriodeviolencia.org.ve/wp-content/uploads/2017/02/UCV-UCAB-USB.-ENCOVI-2016.-Alimentaci%C3%B3n.pdf

[8] http://www.panorama.com.ve/experienciapanorama/Consumo-de-yuca-amarga-ha-matado-a-12-personas-en-los-ultimos-siete-meses-20170125-0006.html
http://www.cnn.com/videos/spanish/2017/03/11/cnnee-pkg-osmary-venezolanos-comen-de-la-basura-crisis-escasez.cnn

[9] http://www.el-nacional.com/noticias/salud/federacion-medica-red-publica-hospitales-esta-bancarrota_43955

[10] http://www.infobae.com/america/america-latina/2017/02/07/trabajadores-de-la-salud-protestaron-en-venezuela-contra-el-abandono-estatal/

[11] http://lat.wsj.com/articles/SB12736863293049773839404582380761769452758

[12] http://www.el-nacional.com/noticias/columnista/ano-2016-colapso-salud-venezuela_72770

6

Corruption and Crime

While many Venezuelans go hungry because they cannot find or pay for basic foodstuffs, the Venezuelan military profits from trafficking in food, as it has been in charge of food distribution since July 2016. "Lately, food is a better business than drugs," said retired Gen. Cliver Alcala, who helped oversee Venezuela's border security. "The military is in charge of food management now, and they're not going to just take that on without getting their cut."[13]

By comparison, however, this would qualify as petty corruption. Precisely, the larger picture is that, according to the US Department of State's 2016 International Narcotics Control Strategy Report, Venezuela is one of the preferred trafficking routes for illegal drugs, predominately cocaine from South America and to a variety of destinations, all facilitated, encouraged, and carried out by its governing elite.[14]

In fact, involvement in drug trafficking reaches the very top of the Venezuelan government. Only so could be explained that Venezuela ranks 7th in private jet ownership.[15] Last February, the U.S. Department of the Treasury designated the Vice-President of Venezuela, Tareck El Aissami, as a "Kingpin Narcotics Trafficker". His primary front-man, Venezuelan national Samark Jose Lopez Bello, was also included in the designation for providing material assistance and financial support, and acting for, or on behalf of, El Aissami.

The Treasury Department further identified and froze assets of 13 companies owned or controlled by Lopez Bello or other designated parties that comprise an international network spanning the British Virgin Islands, Panama, the United Kingdom, the United States, and Venezuela.[16] The freezing of assets blocks the Vice-President from accessing a fortune estimated at $3 billion.[17]

El Aissami is the most recent senior figure in the Venezuelan government to be accused of drug trafficking, but by no means the only one. In August 2016, U.S. prosecutors announced an indictment against two former top officials at Venezuela's anti-narcotics agency. One of those officials, Nestor Reverol, was the former general director of the anti-narcotics agency and onetime commander of Venezuela's National Guard.[18] He was appointed Interior Minister by President Maduro the next day, an obvious move to grant him immunity.

---

[13] Venezuelan Military Trafficking Food as Country Goes Hungry, The Associated Press, December 28, 2016, http://bigstory.ap.org/article/64794f2594de47328b910dc29dd7c996/venezuela-military-trafficking-food-country-goes-hungry

[14] *2016 International Narcotics Control Strategy Report*, US Department of State, Bureau of International Narcotics and Law Enforcement Affairs, https://www.state.gov/j/inl/rls/nrcrpt/2016/vol1/253323.htm

[15] https://www.forbes.com/forbes/welcome/?toURL=https://www.forbes.com/sites/niallmccarthy/2017/03/02/the-countries-where-private-jet-ownership-is-soaring-infographic/&refURL=https://t.co/YZGn09s7lc&referrer=https://t.co/YZGn09s7lc#33bb8302539e

[16] *Treasury Sanctions Prominent Venezuelan Drug Trafficker Tareck El Aissami and His Primary Frontman Samark Lopez Bello*, United States Department of the Treasury, February 13, 2017, https://www.treasury.gov/press-center/press-releases/Pages/as0005.aspx

[17] *US sanctions Venezuelan Vice-President and accuses him of being a drug kingpin*, Miami Herald, February 13, 2017, http://www.miamiherald.com/news/nation-world/world/americas/venezuela/article132494809.html

[18] U.S. indicts ex-Venezuelan anti-narcotics agency leaders on drug charges, Reuters, August 1, 2016, http://www.reuters.com/article/us-venezuela-usa-indictment-idUSKCN10C378

In addition, El Aissami appears to be a key contact in Latin America for extremist organizations. Last February CNN and CNN en Español published a report on an organization created to sell Venezuelan passports. According to CNN, intelligence links Vice President El Aissami to 173 Venezuelan passports and ID's that were issued to individuals from the Middle East, including people connected to the terrorist group Hezbollah.[19]

In November 2015, Efraín Campos and Francisco Flores, nephews of the First Lady, were arrested by DEA agents in Haiti for conspiring to smuggle as much as 1,700 pounds of cocaine into the United States. A year later they were found guilty by a jury in Federal District Court in Manhattan. They each face 10 years in prison.[20] According to news sources, piloting the jet that took the President's nephews to Haiti were members of the presidential security and transportation unit, the Casa Militar.[21] In sum, in Venezuela the ruling elite should be seen as no more than a criminal organization that has managed to capture the state apparatus.

Inevitably, lawlessness from above breeds lawlessness from below. Venezuela experienced 28,000 killings in violent acts throughout the country in 2015, with a rate of 91 murders per 100,000. Since 2014, Caracas has been the most violent city on earth, with a murder rate of 120 per 100,000. Because of this the capital city has a natural curfew, with empty streets after dark.[22]

Regular people fear common criminals as much as law enforcement agents. The latter because either they are themselves engaged in crime—as shown above, smuggling, drug and food trafficking—or because when they do fight urban crime they abuse their power. As reported by a number of human rights organizations, members of the security forces have committed grave violations, including extrajudicial killings, and arbitrary detentions and deportations. As an indicator, from January to June of 2016 extrajudicial killings increased by 66%.[23]

At the same time, 2016 witnessed the highest number of murdered security forces in the past five years with 414 cases, according to a report by the human rights Due Process Foundation (*Fundación para el Debido Proceso - FUNDEPRO*). The report was published in January 2017 and it compiled data from news coverage and interviews with security forces.[24] It has also been documented by other sources that clashes between different smuggling and trafficking gangs formed by members of the security forces also account for some of these killings.

A Call for Action

The Venezuelan regime represents a risk for its own people and the region. Widespread collusion between government officials and criminal organizations—a *narco-state*, we hear often—is a threat

[19] http://www.cnn.com/2017/02/08/world/venezuela-passports-investigation/
[20] *2 Nephews of Venezuela's First Lady Convicted on Drug Charges in U.S. Court*, New York Times, November 18, 2016, https://www.nytimes.com/2016/11/19/world/americas/nephews-of-venezuelas-first-lady-convicted-in-us.html
[21] Venezuela Military Officials Piloted Drug Plane, Insight Crime, November 20, 2015, http://www.insightcrime.org/news-briefs/venezuela-military-officials-piloted-drug-plane
[22] *Caracas World's Most Violent City: Report*, InSight Crime, http://www.insightcrime.org/news-briefs/caracas-most-violent-city-in-the-world-2015-report
[23] https://www.derechos.org.ve/actualidad/cofavic-procedimientos-de-seguridad-ciudadana-ejecutados-por-el-estado-venezolano-estan-incurriendo-en-crimenes-de-lesa-humanidad
[24] http://www.insightcrime.org/news-briefs/venezuela-security-forces-killed-record-numbers-2016

that the countries of the Americas can no longer ignore. Intelligence and journalistic reporting shows that Colombia's ELN (National Liberation Army) and FARC (Revolutionary Armed Forces of Colombia) also operate in Venezuela in coordination with drug cartels. The country has become a smuggling route as much as a safe haven for guerrillas-turned-drug dealers.

The United States has used and should continue to use targeted sanctions against individuals involved in corruption, drug trafficking, money laundering, and human rights violations. The United States should also renew its efforts to build a larger coalition in the region, to persuade governments in Latin America and the Caribbean to cooperate more actively. In July 2014, the government of Aruba released and sent back to Venezuela General Hugo Carvajal, head of military intelligence between 2004 and 2008, after initially detaining him over United States accusations of drug trafficking activities. This was unfortunate. The nations of the hemisphere have to understand that their own national security, public health and financial stability are also at stake.

The claim made by the Maduro regime that these are sanctions against the Venezuelan people is preposterous to say the least. The only sanctions against the people of Venezuela have been issued by the government of Venezuela; namely, by its continuous abuses and its refusal to accept international humanitarian aid to mitigate the effects of dramatic food and medicine shortages. This is a government at war with its own people.

The hardship endured by the Venezuelans also entail the risk of a massive refugee crisis, equivalent to those typically following a war, a natural disaster, or a famine. A large proportion of the country's citizens are already suffering hunger and are victimized by disease and lack of medical attention. Venezuela is a large country in the region—30 million people—bordering Colombia, Brazil and Guyana. Six million Colombians live in Venezuela, many of them having fled from guerrilla and drug trafficking violence in their country of origin.

While there has already been instances of migration, a massive exodus would be a destabilizing factor for Venezuela's neighbors and represent an even larger risk for those—much smaller— countries in the Caribbean basin and Central America. Consider the fact that Panama is already denying visas to Venezuelans, who had been settling there in large numbers over the last few years. This is a collective problem that requires a collective solution.

The Venezuelan government's protracted authoritarianism is a very negative example in the hemisphere. On March 2, 2017 a United States Senate Resolution introduced earlier in February and expressing concern about Venezuela was unanimously approved. That resolution "urges the President of the United States to provide full support for OAS efforts in favor of constitutional and democratic solutions to the political impasse, and to instruct appropriate Federal agencies to hold officials of the Government of Venezuela accountable for violations of United States law and abuses of internationally recognized human rights".[25]

It also "affirms its support for OAS Secretary General Almagro's invocation of Article 20 of the Inter-American Democratic Charter and urges the OAS Permanent Council, which represents all of the organization's member states, to undertake a collective assessment of the constitutional and democratic order in Venezuela".

---

[25] https://www.congress.gov/115/bills/sres35/BILLS-115sres35is.xml

The Inter-American Democratic Charter is an agreement that 34 nations of the Americas signed freely and voluntarily. Doing so, they entered into a commitment to choose plural, constitutional democracy as the only legitimate form of government. The Democratic Charter—*la Carta Democrática*—is binding. It specifies mechanisms for collectively evaluating deviations from the principles of constitutional democracy and collectively choosing paths to restore them.

The government of Venezuela has indeed deviated from those principles. For over a year now, OAS Secretary General Luis Almagro has been delineating a course of action and proposing different steps to do exactly that, all in accordance with Article 20 of the Charter which calls for the "convocation of the Permanent Council to undertake a collective assessment of the situation and to take such decisions as it deems appropriate," including the necessary diplomatic initiatives.

Article 21, in turn, specifies that "when the special session of the General Assembly [of the OAS] determines that there has been an unconstitutional interruption of the democratic order of a member state, and that diplomatic initiatives have failed, the special session shall take the decision to suspend said member state from the exercise of its right to participate in the OAS by an affirmative vote of two thirds of the member states in accordance with the Charter of the OAS."[26]

In other words, when a government ceases to be accountable to its own people, the Democratic Charter holds that government accountable. The Inter-American system has an obligation to hold Maduro accountable on behalf of the Venezuelan people.

We need to put words and actions together. Those sitting on the fence, OAS member states that have been timid and even willing to defer to the whims of the Venezuelan dictatorship, must understand that its constitutional breakdown is a hemispheric security threat. It also sets a bad example, one that would empower other would-be dictators in the region. We should join forces around the Democratic Charter, the most important institutional tool for the collective defense of democracy in the Americas.

---

[26] http://www.oas.org/charter/docs/resolution1_en_p4.htm

Mr. DUNCAN. Thank you, Dr. Schamis.
Now we will go to Dr. McCarthy.

STATEMENT OF MICHAEL MCCARTHY, PH.D., RESEARCH FEL-LOW, CENTER FOR LATIN AMERICAN AND LATINO STUDIES, AMERICAN UNIVERSITY

Mr. McCarthy. Chairman Duncan, Ranking Member Sires, members of the committee, thank you for the invitation to testify today.

Let me begin by commending the committee. This committee has long appreciated the importance of the Venezuela situation, and it has taken steps to raise awareness about the potential negative impacts of the Venezuela crisis on the United States, the hemisphere, and global governance.

It is an honor to join the committee in this ongoing process of discussing policy options and considering potential solutions. I look forward to your advice and questions.

Mr. Chairman, Venezuela's downward spiral has left the country poised between crisis and collapse. As you know, over the last 3 years the economy has fallen into a depression marked by severe shortages and hyperinflation; social protests frequently erupted into episodes of violent instability; and the government dismantled what remained of one of Latin America's oldest democracies, yielding an authoritarian regime.

Maduro and his government are hunkered down. In 2016, the government illegally blocked the opposition's constitutional push for a recall referendum. Then, after Vatican-facilitated international dialogue broke down, the country's humanitarian crisis escalated. Among other illegal detentions, the government arbitrarily jailed an elected Member of Congress. And as the rule of law further collapsed, the number of political prisoners rose to well over 100.

These power grabs amount to a Presidential self-coup. Regrettably, 2017 projects as another year of full-blown crisis. The population is restive and it is suffering amid an emerging humanitarian crisis. Great uncertainty persists about whether postponed gubernatorial elections will take place this year. And if there are no elections in 2017, then the popular response would likely be contentious protests, perhaps including street clashes.

For the hemisphere, the country's current trajectory represents a fundamental threat to its economic, social, and political stability. And I want to stress that today the Venezuela crisis is already a regional one. There are ominous signs out there, and there is already a substantial degree of regional instability.

Over the last 3 years, Colombian civil society groups estimate that had 1.2 million Venezuelans entered the country. The breakdown of the numbers in terms of the type of migration is unclear. What we do know is that overall an estimated 350,000 Venezuelans stayed in Colombia.

In 2016, Venezuelans submitted the most asylum requests of any nationality in three countries: The United States, Brazil, and Spain. In Central America, Costa Rica and Panama have experienced significantly increased levels of migration from Venezuela, while Caribbean countries continue to report high numbers of migration.

In Europe, governments in Italy, Portugal, and Spain are casting a watchful eye over events. There are between 800,000 and 1 million Venezuelans with European Union passports. The overwhelming majority of these passport holders are from these three countries.

The Venezuelan Government is responsible for this manmade disaster, and it will be up to Venezuelans to address the toughest problems, but the international community cannot remain idle. The crisis is already regional in its effects, and sustainable reconstruction will require determined international leadership and well-coordinated assistance efforts.

For the United States, facilitating reconstruction can start with formulating a full-fledged policy for democratic stability in Venezuela. And I want to talk to you about messages, preparations, and actual policy options in the time that is remaining.

The United States can start by sending an important message, in private and in public, that any transition must be peaceful and constitutional or else it will lack legitimacy. It also should send a message by speaking out about the importance of protecting legitimate political spaces. The opposition is under constant harassment, and it is crucial the United States work with regional partners and European allies to protect spaces for civil and political mobilization. Moving along to actual planning options. To address the imme- diate effects of the crisis, the United States should consider options for delivering humanitarian assistance to support the health sector.

This needs to be done through secure multilateral or third-party channels. President Maduro's request for technical medical assistance from the United Nations is not credible. We need evidence of deeds that clearly demonstrate the government's willingness to accept relief via nonpoliticized channels of distribution.

The United States can consider three areas of policy action in the following order. First, I think we need to redouble efforts to apply the Inter-American Democratic Charter, supporting Secretary General Almagro's efforts. And I think it is important that we work with regional governments in the region to bring along those who thus far are not convinced that the application is justified.

At the same time, we need to make clear the cost of nonaction regarding applying the Inter-American Democratic Charter. Not pressing to hold Venezuela to account would set a very bad precedent. In fact, it would send a dangerous message, that those who implement the model of authoritarian government may avoid being held accountable for their actions.

I think that the Trump administration should strongly consider policy continuity with regard to the Caribbean Energy Security Initiative previously led by Vice President Biden. I think that effort is crucial to addressing the structural problem of dependence on subsidized Venezuelan oil.

Now, moving along to the issue of sanctions. I think it is important to recognize that to maximize targeted impact, sanctions need to be seen as a tool, as part of a policy. Their effectiveness ultimately depends on the ability to advance a policy.

In this respect, two questions need to be asked in the context of considering action: Does the measure achieve high targeted impact at a low multilateral cost? And do they raise the costs of the status quo for the government without disproportionately raising exit costs for government leaders.

And I will conclude with one policy option that is new in terms of the policy toolbox out there. In 2016, the Global Magnitsky law came into being as a result of the Defense Authorization Act. My understanding is that it still needs implementing regulations, but the statutory language seems to be pretty clear based on its proto-type. And the innovation with regards to this piece of legislation is that it would allow the United States Government to sanction human rights abusers without also invoking the International Emergency Economic Powers Act, and that is the act that requires the United States Government to declare the situation in a country an unusual and extraordinary national security threat to the United States.

So summing up, if utilized, the Global Magnitsky Act might cre-ate greater clarity about the intention of U.S. sanctions.

Thank you very much.

[The prepared statement of Mr. McCarthy follows:]

Prepared Statement
Dr. Michael McCarthy[1]
Research Fellow
Center for Latin American and Latino Studies
American University
mmccarth@american.edu

House Committee on Foreign Affairs
Subcommittee on the Western Hemisphere
Hearing on "Venezuela's Tragic Meltdown"
1st Session, 115th U.S. Congress
2172 Rayburn House Office Building
March 28, 2017

Chairman Duncan, Ranking Member Sires, Members of the Committee: Thank for you the invitation to testify today.

Let me begin by commending the committee. You have long appreciated the importance of the Venezuelan situation and have duly raised awareness about the potential negative impacts of the Venezuela crisis on the United States, the hemisphere, and global governance.

It is an honor to join the committee in this ongoing process of considering policy options and discussing potential solutions. I look forward to your advice and questions.

Between Crisis and Collapse

Mr. Chairman, Venezuela's downward spiral has left the country poised between crisis and collapse. As you know, over the last three years, the economy has fallen into a depression marked by severe shortages and hyperinflation; social protest frequently erupted into episodes of violent instability; and the government dismantled what remained of one of Latin America's oldest democracies, yielding an authoritarian regime.

President Nicolás Maduro is hunkered down. He has held on through military-tolerated power grabs. His actions amount to a Presidential self-coup.

This has worsened the political crisis. In 2016, Maduro illegally blocked the opposition's Constitutional push for a Recall Referendum. Then, after Vatican- and Union of South American Nations (UNASUR)-sponsored talks between the Maduro Government and the opposition's *Mesa de la Unidad* (The Democratic Roundtable) coalition broke down, the country's human rights crisis escalated. Among other illegal detentions, the government arbitrarily jailed an elected member of Congress. As the rule of law further collapsed, the number of political

---

[1] Adjunct Professor, Elliott School of International Affairs, George Washington University; Founder and Editor, Caracas Wire; Consultant, Latin America Program, Woodrow Wilson Center for Scholars.

prisoners rose to well over one hundred.[2]

2017 projects as another year of full-blown crisis. The population is restive and it is suffering amid an emergent humanitarian crisis. Great uncertainty persists about whether postponed gubernatorial elections postponed will take place this year. If there are no elections in 2017, then the popular response would likely be contentious protests, perhaps including street clashes.

The Crisis Inflection Point

The country's socio-economic descent is the direct result of a failed governance model. That model created the conditions for wastefulness, rampant corruption, and the collapse of the rule of law.

Between 1999 and 2015 the Venezuelan government wasted an oil boom. Over this time period, the government reported $893 billion in petroleum export revenues. Just over half of this total— $450 billion—was earned during the second term of Hugo Chávez, 2007-2012. During Chávez's rule, the conditions for today's crisis emerged. The government ignored fiscal discipline, failed to save oil revenues, and expropriated productive businesses as part of a broader effort to undermine the private sector. When global oil prices collapsed fifty percent in 2015 this shock uncovered the economy's vulnerabilities. Amid a further twenty percent decline in oil prices in 2016, Venezuela's year-on-year oil production fell eleven percent. This equaled a loss of over two hundred thousand barrels a day.

Instead of making economic reforms that might have mitigated the crisis, the Maduro government looked for scapegoats. Maduro accused the United States, the local private sector, and Colombian authorities of waging economic war against the government. As a default measure implemented to help the government pay its foreign debt, the government slashed imports. State imports—which are the main source for food, basic goods, and medicine— declined from $57 Billion in 2012 to $17.6 Billion in 2016.[3]

In 2016, poverty reached eighty percent, and one out of every five Venezuelans reported consuming one meal a day.[4] In the health sector, conditions at hospitals deteriorated steeply. In 2016, seventy six percent of hospitals reported serious scarcities of medicines and eighty one percent faced shortages of medical and surgical supplies.[5] Infant and maternal mortality, malnutrition, and tropical diseases all grew to their highest levels in decades.[6]

In this context, popular support for the government has dramatically declined. According

---

[2] Venezuelan human rights NGO Foro Penal regularly updates data regarding the number of political prisoners. See Foro Penal: https://foropenal.com/presos-politicos/lista-publica.

[3] Michael M. McCarthy, "Venezuela's Manmade Disaster," Current History February 2017.

[4] Venebarómetro, February, 2017; Encuesta nacional de condiciones de vida Venezuela, 2016, http://www.fundacionbengoa.org/noticias/2017/encovi-2016.asp

[5] Observatorio Venezolano de Salud, "Encuesta nacional de hospitales," http://www.ovsalud.org/publicaciones/salud/encuesta-nacional-de-hospitales-2016/

[6] Ibid; Barbara Fraser and Hildegrad Willer, "Venezuela: aid needed to ease the health crisis," The Lancet, Volume 388, No. 10048, September 3, 2016, pp. 947–949.

to a February 2017 Venebarómetro poll, eighty-five percent of the population considers the country's situation negative. Nearly seventy percent would like Maduro to leave power immediately.

The chavista political movement has suffered the consequences of remaining loyal to a failed governance model. Chavismo has lost its luster, its links to state corruption are evident, and its leaders are unpopular. However, it would be premature to characterize the movement as defunct. According to a February 2017 Venebarómetro poll, thirty percent of Venezuelans self-identify as chavistas. Twenty four percent self-identify as members of chavismo's political party, the *Partido Socialista Unida de Venezuela* (PSUV).[7]

With chavismo in decline, the opposition has gained the upper hand in the polls. Its leadership is disjointed. But, following on its landslide victory in the December 2015 National Assembly elections, the anti-government coalition has made significant gains. For example, according to multiple polls, the opposition would win any national election held in Venezuela this year.[8] Its constitutional proposal to recall President Maduro mobilized millions before the government illegally canceled the petitioning process.

At the level of the popular mood, the population is still mourning the loss of the Recall Referendum option. Speaking broadly, the emotional state of the population seems to swing back and forth between growing fed-up and becoming deeply frustrated. In the first quarter of 2017, the country has not seemed to be as much of a powder keg as it was this time last year. However, the possibility of collapse into civil strife still exists.

Regional and Global Dimensions of Venezuela's Crisis

For the hemisphere, the country's current trajectory represents a fundamental threat to its economic, social, and political stability.

Without delay, the hemispheric community must address two challenges.

First, from a political and moral standpoint, the hemisphere must speak out about Maduro's Presidential self-coup. Maduro's actions demand a response at the Organization of American States (OAS), the premier diplomatic forum in the Americas. The organization's *magna carta* for democracy in the Americas, the Inter-American Democratic Charter (IADC), should be applied to hold the Maduro Government to account.[9]

Second, from a security and economic standpoint, the hemisphere must prevent a collapse

---

[7] Venebarómetro, February, 2017.

[8] Alessando di Stasio, "En Venezuela no habrá elecciones mientras la oposición pueda ganar," *Efecto Cocuyo*, February 10, 2017. http://efectococuyo.com/politica/edgard-gutierrez-en-venezuela-no-habra-elecciones-mientras-la-oposicion-pueda-ganar.

[9] Michael M. McCarthy, "The Venezuela Crisis and Latin America's Future: Toward a Robust Hemispheric Agenda on Democratic Stability," Woodrow Wilson Center Latin America Program, March 22, 2017, https://www.wilsoncenter.org/publication/the-venezuela-crisis-and-latin-americas-future?utm_content=buffer334df&utm_medium=social&utm_source=twitter.com&utm_campaign=buffer.

into civil strife. On this front, ominous signs are already visible. In 2016, the Venezuela crisis began to generate instability throughout the region.

In a collapse scenario, neighbor Colombia would experience the most severe direct repercussions. This is of great concern to U.S. interests in South America. While Colombia has made important strides in strengthening state institutions and expanding sovereignty throughout the countryside, it is still in a very fragile place. Confirmation that coca cultivation spiked to 188,000 hectares – a level unseen in two decades – is very alarming.[10] As Colombia begins to implement the peace accord signed with the *Fuerzas Revolucionarias de Colombia* (FARC), it will need substantial assistance to prevent backsliding.

Colombia and Venezuela are sibling nations. They have a recent political history of rivalry and disagreement. But strong cultural ties also link the two countries. There is a sizable Colombian-Venezuelan population and also a history compassionate efforts to integrate migrants from the other country into national society. Civil society groups estimate that 1.2 million Venezuelans entered Colombia in the last three years. An estimated 350,000 remained in Colombia.[11]

In 2016, Venezuelans submitted the most asylum requests of any nationality in three countries: The United States (18,155), Brazil (2,238) and Spain (3,960).[12] In Central America, Costa Rica and Panama have experienced significantly increased levels of migration from Venezuela while Caribbean countries continue to report higher numbers.[13]

In Europe, governments in Italy, Portugal, and Spain are already casting a watchful eye over events. There are between 800,000 and 1,000,000 Venezuelans with European Union (EU) passports. The overwhelming majority of EU passport holders are from these three countries. These countries are already overwhelmed with immigrants from Africa and the Middle East and recent inflows of refugees. At this time, they are especially ill- equipped to absorb a mass inflow of migrants from Venezuela.

Globally, a collapse in Venezuela would likely produce three sets of disruptive effects: financial panic amid an increased chance of debt defaults, oil market volatility from the loss of Venezuelan oil exports, and a deepening of already complex security challenges regarding transnational crime.

---

[10] The Associated Press, "Colombia's coca cultivation soars to highest level in two decades, says US," March 14, 2017. https://www.theguardian.com/world/2017/mar/14/colombia-coca-cocaine-us-drugs.

[11] Javier Molina, "Cada vez es mayor la migración de venezolanos a Colombia," February 5, 2017, http://m.elpais.com.co/colombia/cada-vez-es-mayor-la-migracion-de-venezolanos-a.html

[12] Refugee Freedom Program, "Presentación en audiencia de la CIDH: La crisis de los refugiados venezolanos," March 22, 2017.

[13] There are two important details to underscore about the overall nature of outmigration from Venezuela. One, both Venezuelans of middle-income and lower-income backgrounds have left in search of new beginnings. Two, beyond economic stress, many leave out of fear of political persecution. This includes population groups not often captured in the media spotlight: segments of the urban poor, which have faced increased repression from the Government's highly militarized police units, and whistleblowers, who must take great care to leave quietly.

In financial centers, a collapse would significantly heighten concern about a debt default. With Chinese and Russian state enterprises extending critical loans to Venezuela, both these governments have financial leverage. We do not know the full details of their bilateral financial arrangements. But it seems plausible to assume that Chinese and Russian government-linked companies could make claims on Venezuela's oil assets in the context of a default. Such claims could also include U.S.-based Citgo. The Maduro government recently mortgaged 49.9 percent of the wholly Venezuelan-owned refining company to Russia's Rosneft oil company, in exchange for a loan valued between $1.5 and $1.9 Billion.[14] An investigation by the Committee on Foreign Investment in the United States (CIFIUIS) into this arrangement is of vital importance for determining its potential impact on U.S.-Russia relations.

Commercially, a collapse would roil international oil markets and create challenges for importers of Venezuela's oil. A disruption of Venezuelan oil exports to the United States would have a substantial commercial impact, in particular along U.S. Gulf Coast. But, there would be no broader national security impact. From 2000 to 2016, Venezuelan oil exports to the United States declined roughly fifty percent—1.54 million barrels a day to 796 thousand barrels a day, according to the United States Energy Information Agency.[15] Venezuelan oil now makes up 9 percent of total U.S. imports.

Caribbean and Central American beneficiaries of Venezuela's Petrocaribe policy (2005-Current) stand to lose the most. In the context of suspended oil sales to Petrocaribe beneficiaries, one could expect heightened economic instability in these countries.[16]

For global security, a collapse would provide an important opportunity window for the numerous criminal actors operating in-country. Narcotrafficking interests have penetrated the highest levels of the government and military, police corruption severely undermines the capacity to fight organized crime and reduce the astonishing murder rate of 70 per 100,000,[17] and security forces are seriously hampered in their effort to safeguard borders because informal economic mafias exercise *de facto* control.[18] In a situation of civil strife, the various criminal actors would likely expand their influences over illicit economies and state institutions.

International Engagement: Messages, Plans, and Policy Options

The Venezuelan government is directly responsible for this manmade disaster, and it will be up to Venezuelans to address the toughest problems. But the international community cannot remain idle. The crisis is already regional in its effects and sustainable reconstruction will require coordinated international assistance.

---

[14] Latin American Herald Tribune, "Venezuela's PDVSA Mortgages U.S. Refinery CITGO to Russia's Rosneft," December 2016, http://www.laht.com/article.asp?ArticleId=2427676&CategoryId=10717
[15] United States Energy Information Agency, "Monthly Imports Report," https://www.eia.gov/petroleum/imports/companylevel/
[16] David L. Goldwyn and Cory R. Gill, "The Waning of Petrocaribe? Central American and Caribbean Energy in Transition," Atlantic Council, 2016.
[17] Dorothy Kronick, "How to Count our Dead," July 1, 2016 https://www.caracaschronicles.com/2016/07/01/our-dead/.
[18] Insight Crime, "Venezuela: 2017," http://www.insightcrime.org/venezuela-organized-crime-news

For the United States, facilitating reconstruction can start with formulating a full-fledged policy and strategy for democratic stability in Venezuela. The policy should be rolled out in consultation with Latin American and European allies so that plans can be implemented in a regionally coordinated fashion.

Fortunately, there is a strong foundation from which to begin. The Trump administration can build on the bipartisan Congressional consensus about the significance of Venezuela's crisis, and reaffirm a key pledge. In 2015, the United States pledged to "stand by the citizens of countries where the full exercise of democracy is at risk, such as Venezuela" and "work with all governments that are interested in cooperating with us in practical ways to reinforce the principles enumerated in the Inter-American Democratic Charter (IADC)."[19] This is a crucial message to reiterate in light of Secretary General Luis Almagro's renewed efforts at the OAS to apply the Charter.

Policy Messages

The United States can send four key messages about the Venezuela crisis that, each at the appropriate time and venue.

Underline Support for Peaceful, Constitutional Change

- First, the United States needs to make clear, in public and in private, that any transition must be peaceful and constitutional or else it will lack legitimacy. The Bush administration lent tacit support for the April 2002 coup against Hugo Chávez. That decision was counter-productive. It hurt the U.S. reputation in the region. The Presidential recall could be reactivated, and early Presidential elections could be held as well, though these are unlikely.

Leverage Multilateral Support to Frame the Crisis as Regional and Increase Pressure

- Second, in its conversations with regional partners, the United States should frame the Venezuelan crisis as already posing major instability problems for Latin America, and thus, as representing the largest obstacle to hemispheric progress. The recent March 23 declaration on Venezuela from fourteen hemispheric governments is a positive start. The Trump administration should remain open to diplomatic initiatives that emerge from Latin America and continue raising the Venezuela crisis in Presidential-level conversations.

Speak Out to Protect Legitimate Political Spaces

- Third, with the opposition under constant harassment, it is crucial the United States work with regional partners and European allies to speak out on behalf of protecting arenas for civil and political mobilization. These spaces must be protected to provide for the possibility of a breakthrough solution.

After Judicial Reform is Underway, Move Transitional Justice Front and Center

---

[19] The White House, "National Security Strategy," February, 2015, https://obamawhitehouse.archives.gov/sites/default/files/docs/2015_national_security_strategy_2.pdf.

- Fourth, in 2016, the Venezuelan Congress passed an Amnesty Law, though the Supreme Court ruled the legislation unconstitutional. For a brief moment, the Amnesty Law placed the crucial issue of transitional justice at the top of the agenda. To increase the chances for sustainable change, Venezuela needs to have continued discussions about what peace building entails. Once judicial reforms begin to reduce impunity levels and help rebuild public support for the rule of law, the United States should consider sending a message that it would support transitional justice processes in the event that Venezuelans create them.

Planning and Assisting with Crisis Alleviation

Immediately, the United States can undertake two contingency planning steps.

Explore Humanitarian Assistance Options
- To address the immediate effects of the crisis, the United States should consider options for delivering humanitarian assistance for the health sector. This can be done through secure multilateral or independent channels that third party groups monitor. The United Nations (UN) and multilateral affiliates are one logical option. President Maduro recently request for technical assistance from the United Nations regarding the country's medical shortages. This request is not yet credible. We need evidence of deeds that clearly demonstrate the government's willingness to accept relief via non-politicized channels of distribution.[20] Food assistance is also needed, though the military's control over the distribution system presents enormous challenges for ensuring efficient delivery. In the meantime, the U.S. should reach out to the UN Food and Agricultural Organization (FAO) to present leadership there with an alternative, more realistic picture of ground level conditions than the one being conveyed by the Maduro government. Likewise, the United States should continue contingency planning efforts for two possibilities—debt default and a migration crisis–and expand these to include coordination with Caribbean nations.

Prepare for Reconstruction
- To start work on long-term reconstruction efforts, the United States should enlist government and multilateral agencies to begin work in three areas: 1) planning for economic restructuring; 2) transferring knowledge and lessons about successful cases of judicial reform, including those that involve internationally supported efforts to fight impunity, such as the UN-supported CICIG in Guatemala and the OAS-supported MACCIH in Honduras, and 3) developing a new counter-drug policy for the Andean region that would establish the strategic objective of fostering cooperation between Colombia and Venezuela in the fight against narcotrafficking.

Sequenced Policy Options

The United States can consider three areas of policy action in the following order.

---

[20] Marilia Brochetto, "Venezuela asks UN for help as medicine shortages grow severe," CNN, March 25, 2017. http://www.cnn.com/2017/03/25/americas/venezuela-maduro-un/

1) <u>Marshal a Multilateral Coalition to Defend Democracy and Increase Pressure</u>

<u>Redouble Efforts to Apply the Inter-American Democratic Charter (IADC)</u>
- In the context of Secretary General Almagro's renewed call for applying the Inter-American Democratic Charter (IADC), the United States should work closely with regional allies to ensure the Charter is at the heart of multilateral efforts to protect and promote democracy in Venezuela. The United States might consider working strategically with moderate regional governments that favor applying the Charter. This may enhance efforts to reach out to those that have been less open to the idea of applying the IADC regarding Venezuela's violation of democratic principle and practice. Pursuing the OAS route is not certain to result in attaining the two-thirds vote support to apply the Charter. But, calling for application may have other positive effects, such as strengthening the regional consensus that the Maduro Government is well off the democratic path. This in turn may have broader value for developing new initiatives based on a shared diagnosis of the government's behavior.

<u>Make Clear the Costs of Non-Action Regarding the IADC</u>
- Equally important is the fact that the costs of non-action are high. Not pressing to hold Venezuela to account via the IADC would set a very bad precedent. It would send a dangerous message: those who implement a model of authoritarian governance may avoid being held accountable for their actions.

<u>Strengthen Relations with the Caribbean and Central America</u>
- To strengthen its leadership role in the Caribbean and Central America, the Trump Administration should take a key step in the name of policy continuity. The administration should strongly consider strengthening the Caribbean Energy Security Initiative previously led by Vice President Biden. U.S. efforts to promote alternative energy sources in the Caribbean and Central America remain crucial for developing sustainable solutions to the problem of dependence on subsidized Venezuelan oil.

2) <u>Link Strategic Diplomacy with Sanctions</u>

<u>To Maximize Targeted Impact, Use the Sanction Tool as Part of a Policy</u>
- Targeted sanctions for human rights abuses and public corruption are an important tool in the policy toolbox. But their effectiveness ultimately depends on their ability to advance a policy. Two questions need to be asked in the course of considering sanctions: 1) Does the measure achieve high targeted impact at a low multilateral cost? 2) Do they raise the costs of the *status quo* for the government without disproportionately raising exit costs for key government leaders? Addressing these questions will ensure that the administration carefully weighs the strategic value of imposing sanctions on the Maduro government. It is important to hold Venezuelan authorities to account for criminal actions, human rights violations, and undermining the rule of law. At the same time, the ultimate goal should be moving beyond condemnation to articulating a policy with regional support.

<u>Clarify Regulations for Implementation of the Global Magnitsky Law</u>

- If further sanctions on Venezuelan authorities are deemed necessary, the United States might consider use of the Global Magnitsky law. The 2016-passed law still needs implementing regulations, though the statutory language seems pretty clear based on the precedent of the prototype—the Magnitsky Act created specifically for addressing human rights violations in Russia. The Global Magnitsky Act is in part designed to allow the U.S. government to sanction human rights abusers without having to invoke the International Emergency Economic Powers Act. This is important since this Act possesses the clause that requires an administration to determine that the "situation" in the country in question represents an "unusual and extraordinary national security threat" to the United States. If utilized, the Global Magnitsky law might create greater clarity about the intentions of U.S. sanctions. This may open the door to multilateral coordination of future sanction actions.

Avoid Economic or Sector-wide Sanctions

- The possibility of placing sanctions on the state-owned oil industry in Venezuela constitutes one of the most aggressive measures available for attempting to place pressure on the Maduro government. In 2016, Venezuela exported 796,000 barrels of oil to the United States, crucial cash flow for the Maduro government. Venezuela also imported an estimated 50,000 barrels a day from U.S. sources in 2016. Sanctioning the oil industry would set a major new precedent. Following the precedent set with regards to sanctions on Russian officials for Russian government actions in Ukraine, targeted sanction action against the Venezuelan oil sector would seem to be justified only if the Venezuelan government undertook direct foreign military actions in the territory of a U.S. ally.

Continue International Law Enforcement Regarding Narcotrafficking

- Venezuela's crisis includes the growing influence of narcotrafficking at the highest levels of the government. International law enforcement efforts – which date to 2008 and most recently involved the February 13, 2017 Special Designation of Vice-President Tareck El-Aissami – regarding narcotrafficking need to continue. The transnational crime of narcotrafficking is a national security issue. But, it does not threaten vital U.S. national security interests.

3) Double Down on International Mediation

Reframe the Dialogue's Stakes and Value

- The United States can double down on international mediation by reframing the stakes of dialogue talks and the overall value of the broader dialogue process. Beyond helping Venezuela avoid civil strife, any efforts to promote talks needs to be premised on ending the authoritarian *status quo*. In this respect, change to the *status quo* means guaranteeing the National Assembly its constitutional authorities, liberating political prisoners, and setting dates for the postponed Governor's elections and the 2018-scheduled Presidential.

Recompose the Mediation Team

- An immediate action is to explore options for recomposing the team of mediators that are working with the Vatican to support dialogue efforts. The inclusion of statespersons without electoral politics backgrounds would be highly useful for giving the team of mediators added authority and increased legitimacy within Venezuela. A recomposed team of mediators would not mean the exclusion of UNASUR. A continued role for UNASUR would help the Maduro government, and the South American community, feel as though their voices are included.

Costs of Disengagement

The United States, the governments of the Western Hemisphere, and the international community can take these direct steps to help prevent a collapse and move Venezuela toward democratic stability. But, expectations need to be kept in check. The tools of diplomacy are highly imperfect.

The ability of the hemisphere, the United States, and the European Union to prompt an immediate change in the behavior of the Maduro government is limited.

A full picture of the international factors shaping Venezuela's future requires factoring in geo-economics. Developments in oil markets and the future of Maduro's financial arrangements with China and Russia—Venezuela's two largest bilateral creditors—are the key difference makers. Eventually, bringing China and Russia into the conversation about Venezuela's future will be necessary.

The strong influences that China and Russia exert in Venezuela constitute one of the best arguments for expanding engagement. In this respect, proposed cuts to the State Department budget seem to be at counter-purposes with our national interests. To increase the priority level of the Venezuelan crisis in the hemisphere, and make sustained progress toward reestablishing democratic stability in Venezuela, the United States needs to redouble engagement.

Thank you, I look forward to your questions.

———

Mr. DUNCAN. Thank you.

Votes will be called at 3, so we are going to try to get through as many questions as members can.

Dr. Hanke, we know that there is a glut of oil that has kept prices down. If there is an increase in the price of a barrel of oil, how will that help Venezuela in the short term?

Mr. HANKE. Well, in the short term PDVSA, the state-owned oil company, might actually move from a negative cash flow—they are spending more money than they are actually taking in right now. So they are running a negative cash flow. And they are exploiting their proven reserves at a very slow rate, and the rate is so slow, actually, that the reserves are actually worthless. And the reason they are doing that is that they haven't been able to maintain their production capacity or expand it.

So if the price goes up—I think my models show that the oil prices will probably reach $70 a barrel by the end of the year, which is quite a bit above where we are now, we are a little bit below $50—that would be helpful, but it is just going to be a little bit of a Band-Aid on PDVSA, to directly answer your question. It will help them. The bleeding will slow down, but they will keep bleeding.

This is the worst run state-owned oil company in the world. I have looked at all of these things, and it ranks at the bottom. It takes, to get the median reserve exploited and brought to the ground, almost 200 years in Venezuela. Exxon, it takes 6.8 years. So all these oil companies, the name of the game is, if you have resources, you have got to get them above ground and sell them. Otherwise, they are not worth very much if you just keep them under cover forever and you discount those reserves that you have in the cupboard at, like, 10 percent rate of interest. For Exxon, the present value of the reserves, the average is 46 percent of the price of the wellhead price of oil right now. For Venezuela, PDVSA, it is zero. Zero.

Mr. DUNCAN. The way I look at it, he has got a hungry nation to feed, $10 billion in debt or whatnot, and creditors are going to want some of that money if the oil prices do jump up. So I am assuming that China and Russia will want some of that.

Let me shift gears real quick and just ask Mr. Dallen about Russia. Talking about the debt and the amount of money owed to Rosneft, in the event of a default, which looks all but definite at this juncture, Rosneft and, by operation of the transitive property Russia, would own a majority share of a U.S. corporation. I think you have touched on that in your comments on that as well. Do you think that Rosneft's investment in CITGO and PDVSA is a calculated part of Moscow's strategy to gain power in the region?

Mr. DALLEN. Thank you, Chairman Duncan. And the short answer is yes. Mr. Putin and Mr. Sechin both wrote their graduate theses on using oil as a geopolitical tool. And some of the decisions that Rosneft has made have not been economically rewarding, but they have given them access and control of important markets all over the world, including our allies in Germany, making them the third-largest refiner now in Germany.

We actually don't know how much Russia owns of Rosneft—how much Rosneft owns of CITGO. We know that they have this lien, but we don't know what triggers it. We don't have access to those documents. When they filed the UCC lien, they only had two pages of the contract. I have excerpted one of them in my—part of them in my remarks. We actually don't know what the trigger is. It could already be triggered. We have no idea.

In addition, PDVSA also mortgaged the other half of CITGO by collateralizing some debt when they did a renegotiation of $2.8 billion swapped into a new bond, because they couldn't pay the short-term bond. And so they collateralized that with the other 50 percent of CITGO.

So it is very much possible, and we don't have access to this. The courts are trying to get it. But a CFIUS review would certainly be helpful. Russia may own a majority of those bonds, making them the majority shareholder and owner of CITGO in the United States.

Mr. DUNCAN. Yeah.

Just shifting gears to a completely different topic, Mr. McCarthy, you mentioned the need for humanitarian aid, multinational humanitarian aid. I don't disagree with you there, when I see starving people eating out of dumpsters and hear the stories that we have heard. But we also hear that a lot of that foodstuffs are prioritized. You see the lines of people waiting, but then the apparatchik ends up getting first choice and the bulk of it.

So what kind of assurances do we have that any sort of multinational humanitarian aid would get to where the real problem is, where the rubber meets the road, in a closed Maduro government?

Mr. McCARTHY. Thank you, Chairman.

I agree with you that making progress on delivery of food would be extremely complicated. In fact, that is why I suggested that it would be perhaps more intelligent to use——

Mr. DUNCAN. Let me just ask you this first: Would the Maduro government even be open to a multinational humanitarian aid effort?

Mr. McCARTHY. The answer to that, I think, is no. But I think that there is the possibility of some type of work on a technical front with regards to the health sector. And I don't want to take Maduro's word seriously, because we need to see real deeds that show genuine interest in trying to obtain some relief for the country.

But I think if there is one area where it makes sense to try and press for alleviating the crisis, it is in the health sector, and that is because there are more opportunities for international engagement that would take place with multilateral institutions, and they would also take place outside channels directly controlled by the military. So in the case of food distribution, the Armed Forces control the process from the imports to the delivery; whereas, in the health sector, the role of the military is not as strong.

Mr. DUNCAN. Thank you for that.

I am going to turn to the ranking member.

Mr. SIRES. Can you please tell me—we have been hearing about Venezuela being on the verge of collapse for the last few years. What further can go wrong until it collapses? I mean, they have no food, they have no health, they have no government. What else can happen that it will collapse?

Mr. HANKE. Let me address that first, if I may. This can go on for a long time.

Mr. SIRES. It has been going on for a long time.

Mr. HANKE. Actually, it has been going on for a long time. Even when I was President Caldera's adviser, things were deteriorating massively, and that is why he brought me in to see if something could be done. It turned out he didn't have the political power at the time to make some of the changes that would have probably corrected the situation.

But, at any rate, you have to think of the following. If you go to Yugoslavia, for example, Yugoslavia in January 1994 had an inflation rate in 1 month—this is 1 month—of 313 million percent. So Venezuela is peanuts compared to what was going on in Yugoslavia. It took a Balkan war, bombing in Belgrade, et cetera, et cetera, et cetera, to finally get Milosevic out in 1999. That is a long time.

Now, if you want even a worse case, of course, the inflation rate in November 2008 in Zimbabwe was going so fast that the prices were doubling every 24 hours. And we still have Mugabe. Mugabe has been there over 30 years. Nothing happened. The place spontaneously——

Mr. SIRES. What has collapsed in Venezuela? That is what I am looking for.

Mr. HANKE. Well, I am telling you that if you think it is going to collapse tomorrow, you might have to think a couple of more times, because there are plenty of cases where you have had—— Mr. SIRES.

Look, I don't think—I want to interrupt, because we have to go and vote. I mean, over the years—I have been here now 10 years. For 10 years, I have been hearing about Venezuela. Okay, maybe different grades of how bad it is.

But I just think this is a typical playbook of communists and socialists to lead into a one-man rule. I mean, they get people involved in trying to survive the 24 hours a day that they have no time to think. And I think this is exactly what is happening in Venezuela. And then you have all these other external forces basically managing Venezuela and their moves.

Mr. HANKE. You hit the nail on the head. I completely agree with you.

Mr. SCHAMIS. If I may add, I don't know what the definition of collapse would be that we are discussing here, but to me the next step and the real collapse is a refugee crisis, which we haven't seen yet.

Mr. SIRES. Well, I spoke to the President of Costa Rica the other day. He is telling me——

Mr. SCHAMIS. The President of Costa Rica——

Mr. SIRES [continuing]. He is starting to see a number of Venezuelans.

Mr. SCHAMIS. Exactly, and all countries around Venezuela. A refugee crisis in Venezuela, we are talking about a 30 million people country, it is not a small island in the Caribbean, countries which have had a refugee crisis, a number of them. This is a country on the continent and a 30 million people country with borders with in turn large countries, Colombia——

Mr. SIRES. I am going to let somebody else. But, Mr. McCarthy, can you just be short?

Mr. McCARTHY. Yes, I will be short. I think collapse entails civil strife. I think at this point it is relative. By most standards, Venezuela has collapsed. At this point, it is about preventing open civil strife in the country.

Mr. SIRES. Thank you.

Mr. DUNCAN. All right. Just trying to stay in order here. Looks like Mr. Rooney.

Mr. ROONEY. Thank you.

There are a lot of questions I would like to ask. First of all, maybe Professor Schamis or Russell.

Given the fact that all the countries of the region except Salvador, Nicaragua, Ecuador, and Bolivia recently denounced Venezuela, which was a positive move, and talked about, even raised the specter of, as a last resort, kicking them out of the OAS. If the OAS is incapable of moving them forward, what do you think of odds of that happening are?

Mr. SCHAMIS. The odds are higher than they were in June, the last meeting of the Permanent Council to discuss Venezuela, because of a variety of circumstances. First and foremost, Venezuela has gotten worse.

Secondly, there is a new administration in the U.S. that has begun to voice concern about Venezuela. It is reported in the newspapers that President Trump discusses Venezuela whenever he is on the phone with Latin American Presidents, which hadn't happened before, we must recognize.

Lastly, there is a change of cycle in the politics of Latin America. Center government, center-right governments you may say, have been winning office and are expressing more concern with Venezuela, who, in turn, are less dependent on the Venezuelan old tricks. With the oil over $130 per barrel, that drove Hugo Chavez's foreign policy and later Maduro's foreign policy. Oil is not $130 per barrel, and those new governments are less dependent. They have less ties, strings attached to the Venezuelan regime.

So the odds are better than they were before, and I am hopeful the OAS will increase its capacity for collective action regarding Venezuela.

Mr. DUNCAN. Got one more?

Mr. ROONEY. We need to get everybody, Chairman, because we don't have much time left. I would yield to someone else.

Mr. DUNCAN. Mrs. Love.

Mrs. LOVE. Thank you. I wish we could spend so much more time on Venezuela. But I guess my question would be, and anyone who can offer the best opinion that they can in terms of correcting human rights abuses and releasing political prisoners, what kind of pressures from the U.S. do you think would be most likely to help?

I know we are talking about sanctions. We talked about some of these other tools. And at this point I believe we are in a place where anything that we do is going to affect the people that are there. But their needs are so incredibly dire that unless there are some major disruptions, nothing is going to be changed.

So I guess I am asking, what are the tools that we have in our arsenal in order to change the environment there, first of all, to release American prisoners, and second of all, to start seeing a little bit of change in the government?

Mr. McCARTHY. Let me try this. Thank you. It is a very difficult question, but it is absolutely urgent, I agree.

The truth is that if you were trying to establish a link between implementation of sanctions and then change in behavior, thus far there is not a positive link. But that doesn't mean that there isn't another effect taking place. So I think, unfortunately, I would counsel patience with regards to the broader human rights situation in the country. I think that it is going to take some time before these problems can be fully addressed because, unfortunately, the government sees the human rights situation as part of a broader political negotiation.

Mrs. LOVE. What about the immediate?

Mr. McCARTHY. With regards to Mr. Holt, I think that that is a private matter, and that has to be dealt with in terms of how the family and the U.S. Government are addressing it.

Mrs. LOVE. Okay. So we have tried quite a bit with the former administration, and it hasn't been moving. We have an American citizen who is there on charges. So I guess what I am trying to say is that I cannot accept that the United States Government can't do anything. I cannot accept that. In terms of if we can't squeeze or try and do everything we can with Venezuela, what about the other countries, some of the ones that we were talking about, that have not denounced Venezuela yet? What about their friends and their allies, like El Salvador, Nicaragua, Ecuador, and Bolivia? Is there a way to actually do that?

Mr. McCARTHY. I think that there has been quite a bit of discussion about what strengthening sanctions would entail, and I think the truth is that multilateral sanctions tend to be more effective than unilateral ones. And I think in that regard the Global Magnitsky Act is one option to think about a way to bring other countries on board, to see if there could be a statement, not just from the United States but from other Latin America countries as well, speaking out about the human rights crisis in Venezuela, which has to be dealt with in terms of results for this American citizen that has unlawfully been jailed.

Mrs. LOVE. Okay.

Do you have an opinion on this, Dr. Schamis?

Mr. SCHAMIS. Yes. Thank you. Briefly, something else the U.S. can do and has happened yesterday or the day before is to enlarge the coalition in support of the Inter-American Democratic Charter and the possibility of suspension or any other form of approach toward Venezuela, which has already been going on, and it has been mentioned. And more members will have more capacity to put pressure on Venezuela.

Whether that is going to be suspension or any other decision remains to be seen. But the bottom line is produce an election, release political prisoners, and attend the humanitarian crisis in a reasonable amount of time.

Mrs. LOVE. And I would actually say that we need to start looking at the U.N., because here we are. They have a seat at the table.

Yet they do not have elections. They do not have freer treatment. They are the worst when it comes to human rights violations. Why they have a seat at the table is beyond me.

So thank you.

Thank you, Mr. Chairman.

Mr. DUNCAN. I want to thank Ms. Love for being here, and with that kind of passion for the subject, you are welcome back to any committee hearing we have any time. So thank you.

I want to thank the panelists. I apologize, with 4 minutes and 40 seconds left on the clock over at the Capitol, we are going to have to go vote. And with about an hour worth of votes, I am not going to ask you to sit here that long and wait for questions.

Members may have additional questions for you, and if they do, we will submit those and ask you to submit answers in writing.

Pursuant to committee rule 7, the members of the subcommittee will be permitted to submit written statements to be included in the official hearing record. Without objection, the hearing record will remain open for 5 business days to allow those statements, questions, extraneous materials for the record, subject to length limitations in the rules.

There being no further business, again I do apologize, but let me reiterate, this is not the last hearing we are going to have on this subject. Venezuela is important to the United States Congress, and it is important to the chairman of the Western Hemisphere Subcommittee. We want to do what we can to keep awareness raised for the Nation and the world to the plight of the people in Venezuela.

And with that, we will stand adjourned.

[Whereupon, at 3:12 p.m., the subcommittee was adjourned.]

APPENDIX

MATERIAL SUBMITTED FOR THE RECORD

SUBCOMMITTEE HEARING NOTICE
COMMITTEE ON FOREIGN AFFAIRS
U.S. HOUSE OF REPRESENTATIVES
WASHINGTON, DC 20515-6128

Subcommittee on the Western Hemisphere
Jeff Duncan (R-SC), Chairman

TO: MEMBERS OF THE COMMITTEE ON FOREIGN AFFAIRS

You are respectfully requested to attend an OPEN hearing of the Committee on Foreign Affairs, to be held by the Subcommittee on the Western Hemisphere in Room 2172 of the Rayburn House Office Building (and available live on the Committee website at http://www.ForeignAffairs.house.gov):

DATE: Tuesday, March 28, 2017

TIME: 2:00 p.m.

SUBJECT: Venezuela's Tragic Meltdown

WITNESSES: Mr. Steve Hanke
                   Co-Director
                   Institute for Applied Economics, Global Health, and the Study of Business Enterprise
                   The Johns Hopkins University

                   Mr. Russell M. Dallen, Jr.
                   President and Editor-in-Chief
                   Latin American Herald Tribune

                   Hector Schamis, Ph.D.
                   Adjunct Professor
                   Walsh School of Foreign Service
                   Georgetown University

                   Michael McCarthy, Ph.D.
                   Research Fellow
                   Center for Latin American and Latino Studies
                   American University

By Direction of the Chairman

The Committee on Foreign Affairs seeks to make its facilities accessible to persons with disabilities. If you are in need of special accommodations, please call 202/225-5021 at least four business days in advance of the event, whenever practicable. Questions with regard to special accommodations in general (including availability of Committee materials in alternative formats and assistive listening devices) may be directed to the Committee.

COMMITTEE ON FOREIGN AFFAIRS

MINUTES OF SUBCOMMITTEE ON _____ *the Western Hemisphere* _____ HEARING

Day __*Tuesday*__ Date __*March 28, 2017*__ Room ____*2172*____

Starting Time __*2:00 PM*__ Ending Time __*3:12 PM*__

Recesses |_*n/a*_| (___to___) (___to___) (___to___) (___to___) (___to___) (___to___)

Presiding Member(s)

Chairman Jeff Duncan (SC-03)

Check all of the following that apply:

Open Session ☑   Electronically Recorded (taped) ☑
Executive (closed) Session ☐   Stenographic Record ☑
Televised ☑

TITLE OF HEARING:

Venezuela's Tragic Meltdown

SUBCOMMITTEE MEMBERS PRESENT:

Chairman Jeff Duncan, Ranking Member Albio Sires, Rep. Ron DeSantis, Rep. Ted S. Yoho, Rep. Francis Rooney, Rep. Joaquin Castro, Rep. Norma Torres, Rep. Adriano Espaillat

NON-SUBCOMMITTEE MEMBERS PRESENT: *(Mark with an * if they are not members of full committee.)*

Rep. Mia Love

HEARING WITNESSES: Same as meeting notice attached? Yes ☑ No ☐
(If "no", please list below and include title, agency, department, or organization.)

STATEMENTS FOR THE RECORD: *(List any statements submitted for the record.)*

none

TIME SCHEDULED TO RECONVENE _____
or
TIME ADJOURNED __*3:12 PM*__

Subcommittee Staff Associate